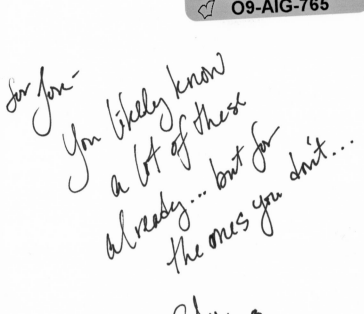

For Jon—

You likely know
a lot of these
already... but for
the ones you don't...

E Ju 2013

THE
WHATCHAMACALLIT

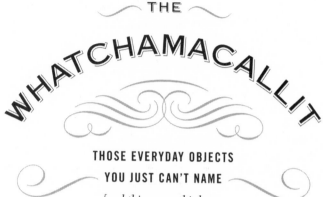

THE
WHATCHAMACALLIT

THOSE EVERYDAY OBJECTS
YOU JUST CAN'T NAME

*[and things you think you
know about but don't]*

DANNY DANZIGER
and
MARK McCRUM

HYPERION

NEW YORK

Library of Congress Cataloging-in-Publication Data is available upon request.

ISBN: 978-1-4013-2338-7

Hyperion books are available for special promotions and premiums. For details contact the HarperCollins Special Markets Department in the New York office at 212-207-7528, fax 212-207-7222, or email spsales@harpercollins.com

FIRST EDITION

Book design by Judith Stagnitto Abbate / Abbate Design

10 9 8 7 6 5 4 3 2 1

SUSTAINABLE FORESTRY INITIATIVE

Certified Fiber Sourcing

www.sfiprogram.org

THIS LABEL APPLIES TO TEXT STOCK

We try to produce the most beautiful books possible, and we are also extremely concerned about the impact of our manufacturing process on the forests of the world and the environment as a whole. Accordingly, we made sure that all of the paper we used has been certified as coming from forests that are managed to insure the protection of the people and wildlife dependent upon them.

CONTENTS

C

D

E

F

G

H

I

J

K

L

M

N

O

P

R

S

T

U

V

W

Y

Z

HOW THIS BOOK CAME ABOUT

The pair of us were having one of our occasional lunches out. For two professional screen slaves, these provide a welcome break from the solitary business of writing. On this particular occasion, at some new restaurant that Danny had discovered in town, we were halfway through our meal when Danny leaned forward and pointed at Mark's upper lip.

"You've got a splash of gravy on your, er . . ."

Mark dutifully wiped the spot with a napkin.

"No, not your lip, just above . . ."

"My nose?"

"No, the bit below your nose, above your lip, on your, your . . . whatchamacallit."

Neither of us, it turned out, knew the word for that intriguing bit of face between the bottom of the nose and the top of the lip. Being mildly obsessive wordsmiths, we had to find out. A day later, Danny phoned Mark with the answer, which he'd learned from his doctor friend Rob. Philtrum. Cary Grant had a long one. Adolf Hitler and Charlie Chaplin covered theirs with a mustache. Hard-eyed marines can, apparently, tap you there in a certain way and kill you. We were both happy to know the right word for this whatchamacallit.

"And Mark," continued Danny, "I was just thinking . . ."

And so this book was born. As Danny pointed out, our world is littered with things we ought to know the names for, quite often nearly know the names for, but, in the end, we don't. Whatchamacallits. Thingamajigs. Doohickeys. Once we started to think about it, there were so many out there.

Now, we didn't want to get sidetracked by the many extraordinary and unlikely terms for things that are used by specialists. Surgeons know their **bistoury** from their **snare**, their **endoscope** from their **speculum**, just as steam-engine enthusiasts know their **flywheel** from their **piston rod** and their **slide valve** from their **steam inlet.** But these, we felt, were not strictly whatchamacallits, because no ordinary person is likely to be called upon to use them.

No, whatchamacallits, we decided, had to be those things that we see, touch, and use every day. Which are between our fingers and under our noses—and yet we cannot put a name to them.

Many are objects. The **dongle** you plug into a computer, the **aglet** at the end of your shoelace. Some are things we barely notice we are using, such as the **keeper** on a belt or the **cradle switch** on a telephone. Others are things that we see around us but have never thought to learn the name for: the **lunula** on a fingernail, the **phloem bundles** of a banana, the **cutwater** on a bridge.

As we thrashed out our long list, and then argued our way down to a short list, we realized that, quite often, one person's whatchamacallit is another person's favorite, most familiar object. A darts player knows their **oche**, just as a doglover knows whether their pet has **dewclaws**. But do either of them know what a **desire line** is or where to look for **drupelets**? And could they tell the difference between a **gnomon** and a **grawlix**?

It is for people such as this—by which we mean pretty much everyone, ourselves included—that we've written this little book. It is not intended as a strenuous study course, more as a laid-back perusal, perhaps in the bath or the smallest room in the house. Miraculously, this will transform you from someone who is occasionally lost for words to that far more dynamic person who—obviously in an understated and discreet sort of fashion—always knows the right word for everything.

Along the way you may start to feel some shame that you didn't know this stuff earlier. Most of us eat three meals a day, with knife, fork, and spoon, yet how many of us know what actually spears the food and gets it up into our mouth? The **tines** of a fork, of course. Those seeds that decorate the outside of a strawberry? **Achenes**. There are, on average, two hundred of them per fruit. Once one has the word at one's fingertips, it seems inconceivable—and almost sad—that one might have gone through the rest of life without learning it.

As we grow older, of course, more and more things

become whatchamacallits. Chefs who once knew their **coquille** from their **cocotte** and their **bain-marie** from their **brochette** will get to a point in life where, even if they can remember the correct word, they can't necessarily be bothered to use it. At that point, the tried and tested line, "Could you pass me the, that, er . . . whatchamacallit," becomes all too useful.

Eventually, for some of us, comes that sad moment when pretty much everything is a whatchamacallit—even, perhaps, our nearest and dearest. Before we reach that stage, and in celebration of the wonderful range of terms that exist to describe specific things in our daily life, here is our selection of whatchamacallits.

ACHENES (pronounced *a-keens*) are the tiny yellow seeds in a strawberry's skin. The average strawberry has around two hundred achenes.

Actually, botanically speaking, the achenes *are* the fruit; the strawberry is simply the receptacle into which the fruits are embedded.

In medieval times, strawberries were regarded as an aphrodisiac, and soup made of strawberries, borage, and soured cream was traditionally served to newly-weds at their wedding breakfast. The strawberry as we know it today came about by chance, after the cross-pollination of two native American strawberries: the scarlet Virginia strawberry from North America, and the Chilean strawberry—as large as a walnut, with a delicate aroma and a pale, almost white flesh. It was a match made in heaven. The Chilean strawberry gave size and firmness to the new fruit, while the wild Virginia strawberry added flavor.

Jean-Baptiste de la Quintinie, the reclu-sive ex-lawyer who was gardener to Louis XIV, is credited with being the first to grow this hybrid in Europe. He was a pioneer of early cultures, producing lettuce in January and strawberries in March, as well as introducing such exotic newcomers as figs and melons to the royal table.

Strawberries contain more vitamin C pound for pound than oranges, and are high in fiber, low in calories, and a good source of both iron and folic acid. Once picked, strawberries don't ripen further, so you should eat them before they rot. Make sure, when choosing your berries, to pick out those with a good, healthy red color, and always with their leafy stem—the **calyx**—firmly attached (once this is removed, an enzyme that destroys vitamin C is released). If any of the berries has mold, avoid the whole container; the chances are the spores will have spread throughout.

An **AGLET** (or *aiglet*) is that little plastic or metal tube at the end of your shoelace.

The aglet's purpose is to stop the thread of the lace from unraveling, as well as to make it easier to feed through the shoe's eyelets. (The word comes from the Old French *aguillette*, which is the diminutive of *aguille*, meaning needle.)

Aglets go back a long way. Before the invention of plastic, they were made of metals like copper, brass, and silver; glass; and even stone. They were often ornamental and some were fashioned into small figures. (In Act I of Shakespeare's *Taming of the Shrew*, Petruchio's servant Grumio talks of marrying him off to "a puppet or an aglet-baby.")

Should your aglet break, you may, of course, just buy another shoelace. But if you're a more frugal kind of person, the aglet can be easily repaired. Shoemakers recommend the following methods:

- dripping candle wax or resin onto the broken end
- soaking the lace end with glue or nail polish
- binding the lace end with fine thread over glue (known as "whipping")
- winding adhesive tape around the lace end

- replacing the broken aglet with heatshrink or small-gauge metal tubing, used respectively by electricians and hobbyists

Before you tie those laces and walk off, turn your shoe over slowly and consider the other parts for which you may well not know the names. Of course, we all know the sole—the bottom of the shoe; and the insole—the interior bottom of the shoe, to which extra insoles may be added, to make the shoe fit tight, or even perhaps just to soak up sweat. But what about the **vamp**, the front of the **upper** of the shoe, crucial in holding the shoe on to the foot. In the case of a sandal or flip-flop (or "thong," as the Aussies call it), this may be just a couple of leather straps.

The **quarter** is the name for the sides and back part of the shoe, and the **throat** is the central part of the vamp leading down to the **toe box**, **cap**, or **puff**. The top of the shoe, where leather meets sock, is the **topline**, and the **welt** is the ridge that runs along the top of the **outsole**, where it's not covered by the upper.

Men's shoes have two main lacing styles, which relate to their construction. With Oxford-style lacing, the eyelet section is part of the quarter, while the **tongue** below is part of the vamp. In the Gibson style, the lacing section is part of the vamp.

GRUMIO: Nay, look you, sir, he tells you flatly what his mind is: Why give him gold enough and marry him to a puppet or an aglet-baby; or an old trot with ne'er a tooth in her head, though she have as many diseases as two and fifty horses: why, nothing comes amiss, so money comes withal.

(*The Taming of the Shrew*, Act I, scene 2)

An **ALLEN WRENCH** is an L-shaped six-sided wrench, which can drive a bolt or screw very tightly into a recessed hexagonal socket hole. It's also known as an Allen or hex **key.**

It is just one of the very useful tools on the new Wenger Swiss Army Knife, called the Giant Collector's Knife, which has eighty-seven implements.

Aside from two 4-mm Allen wrenches, this bristling behemoth has—to highlight just some of its features—a dozen or so blades, three types of pliers, and countless screwdrivers, including a screwdriver specifically for gun sights. It has an implement designed to tighten spikes on a golf shoe. It has saws. It has a reamer, which is a tool to make or enlarge holes, and another tool just for opening the case of a watch. It has a bicycle-chain rivet setter, a signal whistle, cigar-cutting scissors, a laser pointer, a torch, a tire-tread gauge, magnifiers, a fish descaler, nail clippers and a nail file, plus the requisite toothpick and tweezers.

For the avid gardener, there are four different blades for grafting one plant onto another.

It also has a keyring at one end—although you're not likely to lose your keys if this monster is attached. The knife weighs two pounds and eleven ounces, and is just under nine inches wide.

ANDIRONS are the cast-iron stands on which logs are laid for burning in a fireplace or grate.

In the past, andirons were used for cooking, with uprights to hold spits, and attached arms or hobs to keep stewpots and casseroles hot. Nowadays, they are just as often placed in front of the hearth, and used to prop up tongs and pokers, small shovels, and brushes.

Andirons are also sometimes called **fire-dogs**, because during the Middle Ages blacksmiths often made them in the shape of hunting dogs. By the time of Louis XIV (1643–1715), the simple andiron had become elaborately ornate, inlaid with gold and silver, and patterned with fleur-de-lis and heraldic ornaments.

An **ARCHITRAVE** is the plain or molded section above (or around) a window or door. But also—and originally—in classical architecture, architrave is the term for the main beam that rests across the tops of the columns of a temple.

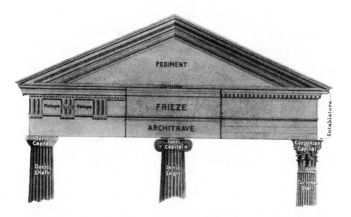

Above the architrave comes the **frieze**, which generally consists of alternating ridged and plain blocks of stone known as **triglyphs** and **metopes**. On top of that is the **cornice**, which completes the **entablature**, as this external upper section of a Greek temple is known. This may, in

turn, be surmounted by a triangular section, the **pediment**,
which may include within it
sculptural decoration known
as the **tympanum**.

The precise structure of the
entablature is different in each of the
three classical Greek orders of architecture: Doric, Ionic, and Corinthian.
The proportions of the entablature relate strictly to those of
the columns, and vary according to the order. In the Ionic
order, for example, the height of the architrave is half the
diameter of the column base; and the dimensions of the rest
of the entablature are calculated as fractions of this measurement.

The Doric order came first, invented in the second half
of the seventh century BC, possibly in the Greek city of
Corinth. Simple, baseless columns rose direct from the
raised **stylobate** (floor) up to a spreading **capital**—the con-
vex **echinus** supporting the square **abacus**. Cognoscenti of
classical architecture may luxuriate further in a wonderful
range of terms for other features of this style: along the top
edge of the architrave runs the narrow **fillet**, or **taenia**; below that, matching the width of the triglyphs, are **tenons**
(or **regulae**), from which, in turn, hang rows of stone **pegs**
(or **guttae**). The most famous Doric building in the world is
the Parthenon.

The more exotic Ionic order evolved at much the same
time in the Greek cities of Asia Minor. Columns were taller
than Doric ones, with capitals consisting of carved **scrolls**,

or **volutes**. They sat on elaborate bases, made up of a square **plinth**, which was surmounted by layers of double roundels and **scotiae** and then the decorated **torus**. Ionic columns also incorporated a new architectural feature called **entasis**—a bulge in the column to make it look straight to the naked eye.

The Corinthian order came later, in the fourth century BC. Now the fluted columns were topped with capitals featuring carved flowers and acanthus leaves below a much smaller scroll, the **helix**.

The Romans used all three of the Greek orders and added two more of their own, the decorative Composite and the simple Tuscan.

These five famous classical orders are not just of interest when one is wandering around the ancient temples of the Mediterranean. Many of the buildings we see around us today have some classical elements, even if they are not completely **neoclassical**. Look up as you pass along a street. The simplest window may have nothing but a sill, but many are surrounded by architraves and some may be topped by cornices. Following the classical original, a frieze may be introduced, or the cornice may be topped with a pediment. A really elaborate window may feature a full order of **colonettes** rising from a bracketed sill, surmounted by a completely pedimented entablature.

Until the start of the twentieth century, architects generally possessed a familiarity with classical architecture, but this diminished as the Modern Movement became established. Modern architects deliberately avoided classical forms, on the grounds that they had become sterile and overused. By the 1950s, classicism seemed finished. Classical solutions to architectural competitions were not taken seriously. Much of the work of the great postwar building boom in Britain reflected this lack of interest in neoclassical forms.

But the ugliness and unpopularity of many of these buildings led eventually to a reigniting of the interest in classical forms. In 1992, after a successful series of annual Summer Schools in Civil Architecture, Prince Charles established his Institute of Architecture to promote classical and counter-Modernist architectural values in the United Kingdom. He had earlier dubbed a proposed extension of the National Gallery in London's Trafalgar Square "a monstrous carbuncle on the face of a much-loved and elegant friend" and suggested that the rubble left by the Luftwaffe had been less "offensive" than the architecture of certain contemporary city buildings.

ARCUATE VANES are the concentric raised ridges running around the top of your Frisbee.

Arcuate simply means bowed or arched. After a botched catch, the roughness of the vanes is the cause of that most common and painful of Frisbee sporting injuries—the Frisbee finger. The aerodynamic reason for their presence is that the vanes near the leading edge act as **turbulators**, which force the airflow to become turbulent after it passes over them, which in turn reduces **flow separation** and thus improves the Frisbee's flight.

The Frisbee's origins can be traced back to a bakery, of all things. In 1871, in the wake of the U.S. Civil War, William Russell Frisbie moved to Bridgeport, Connecticut, to manage a branch of the Olds Baking Company of New Haven. He made such a success of the place that he soon bought it outright and named it the Frisbie Pie Company. Under his direction, and subsequently that of his son, Joseph P. Frisbie, the small company prospered and grew to an empire of 250 shops. Their most popular items were the Frisbie Pies, which were sold along with their tin baking dishes (a five-cent deposit was refunded if you returned the dish).

Students at nearby Yale then discovered that these baking tins could sail through the air, albeit with a wobbly and unpredictable trajectory, and soon you couldn't walk past a college building without being clocked on the head by one.

Some time in the mid 1940s, a businessman and inventor called Walter Morrison decided to develop the recreational possibilities of these grown-up toys, designing the world's first plastic flying disc, which he called the Whirlo-Way. This he followed in 1955 with a disc that exploited the public's interest in UFOs by looking like a flying saucer—the Pluto Platter.

In 1956, Morrison sold the Platters idea to Ed Headrick at Wham-O, who improved the aerodynamics of the discs by building in arcuate vanes. He called his version Rings of Headrick, but this name didn't catch on. They were universally known as Frisbees, even though the original pie company had gone out of business.

By the early 1970s, Ultimate Frisbee, a non-contact team game for two teams of seven people, was being played all over the world. Today, you can still hardly visit a college campus, playground, or stretch of beach where you won't see a Frisbee being tossed around by devoted Frisbyterians.

The **AT SIGN** was originally an abbreviation of the phrase "at the rate of" and was incorporated as a standard key on the earliest typewriter keyboards. Its official typographic nomenclature is **commercial at**.

For a while, in the late twentieth century, when mental arithmetic was being replaced by calculators, and schoolchildren no longer learned how to tally up the price of 30 apples @ 5¢ an apple, it looked as if the dear old @ sign might die out entirely.

However, a rescue was in the offing. In 1971 an American computer programmer named Ray Tomlinson, who was working at BBN Technologies in Cambridge, Massachusetts, on an inter-user mail program called SNDMSG, sent the world's first e-mail, between two computers that were sitting side by side. Needing to distinguish the name of the user from the name of the computer the user was working at, he decided to reassign the @ sign, so that it now referred to location rather than rate. "Don't tell anyone," he is said to have instructed a colleague to whom he showed his invention. "This isn't what we're supposed to be working on." Thirty years later, the use of @ in e-mail is universal.

As most languages didn't use the @ sign before the arrival of e-mail, it has earned itself a range of interesting local nicknames. In Polish, it is *malpa*, monkey, while the Dutch call it *apestaart*, monkey's tail. In Danish, it is *snabel*, elephant's trunk, or *grisehale*, pig's tail. The Hungarians call it *kukac*, maggot, and the Italians *chiocciola*, the snail. For the Koreans, too, it's the snail (*dalphaengi*), while for speakers of Mandarin in China or Taiwan it's *xiao laoshu*, little mouse. The Thais are less specific, calling it *'ai tua yiukyiu*, the wiggling, wormlike character. In Turkey, it's *kulak*, ear, and in the Czech Republic, *zavináč*, rollmop herring. The Swedes also have a food nickname, *kringla*, pretzel, but this is just one of a number of names, ranging from *elefantora*, elephant's ear, through *apsvans*, monkey's tail, to *kattfot*, cat-foot, and *kattsvans*, cat's tail.

A **BAIN-MARIE** is a double saucepan in which a working liquid, typically water, surrounds sauce or other food, which then can be heated more gently and steadily than by naked flame or raw electric element.

Bain-maries are typically used to make such sauces as Hollandaise or *beurre blanc*, which might curdle at a harsher heat. Chocolate sauce, egg custard, and lemon curd are also often made in the bain-marie, while oven-cooked dishes such as cheesecake or terrines may be baked sitting in a pan of water to control the temperature—another manifestation of the bain-marie. The word can refer to something as simple as a china bowl sitting over a saucepan of boiling water; any kind of bain-marie can be used to keep things warm, just as much as for cooking.

The bain-marie is no faddish luxury of the modern world, like the blender or the electric lettuce dryer. Its invention is generally credited to Maria the Jewess (also Maria Hebraea, Maria Prophetissa), a chemist of ancient times, who some sources say was Miriam, the sister of Moses, and others a Syrian princess, who visited the court of Alexander the Great and learned the art of making gold from Aristotle. Whatever the truth of the legends, she was undeniably a real person, who wrote about the methods and equipment of alchemical operations, several of which required the gentle heat of her double saucepan, to mimic the process by which precious metals were originally formed in the earth's crust.

Other utensils around the kitchen that are familiar to the chef but not always known to the amateur cook are:

- the **brochette,** the small skewer or spit on which chunks of meat are cooked
- the **mandoline,** the vegetable slicer with the adjustable blade
- the **ramekin,** the small ovenproof dish, in which appetizers and desserts are often served as individual portions
- the **timbale**, the cup-shaped mold used for rice or exotic cold appetizers
- the **zester**, the specialized tool that whips off the **zest,** the outer, colored skin of citrus fruit

The French, incidentally, use the word as a slang term for a woman with more looks than brains: *une femme au bain-marie*—a woman with a double saucepan for a head.

The **BAISEMAIN** is a light kiss on the hand. It's a tradition perfected primarily by the Frenchman of a certain age, who has been versed from his earliest years in the black arts of charm and seduction.

Performed and executed in just a few moments, it's a tricky physical maneuver, which requires the man simultaneously to click his heels, bow at the waist and neck, and then pick up the lady's hand, the back of which he lightly and briefly touches to his lips. This apparently innocent act seems to be irresistibly attractive to American women. Unfortunately, it looks ridiculous when performed by an American or Anglo-Saxon male, so it's probably best to leave it to our Gallic cousins.

Another type of kiss, important to the French, is the kiss on the cheek, known as **la bise**. How many kisses you should bestow is hotly debated. In certain parts of the country, the quick left-right double kiss is simply not considered enough. Three, four, and sometimes even five cheek kisses are required as an essential staple of etiquette.

A **BESOM** (pronounced *beez-om*) is the archetypal witch's broomstick, where a cluster of twigs is tied to a long wooden stick. It was once said that witches disguised their wands as besoms.

In ancient times, besoms were used in every home, and became a symbol of household cleanliness—even though their rounded shape was quite inefficient for sweeping. The Saxons even had besom squires, craftsmen who reserved particular coppices where birch and ash for the handles grew profusely. Branches of broom were used to make the sweeping-heads; hence broom, a word these besoms came to be known by.

In the early nineteenth century, the Shakers developed the flat broom, which had a far more effective shape for pushing dust and dirt, and immediately caught on. Eventually this put an end to the English be-som industry (although Thomas Hardy's *The Return of the Native* (1878) includes a character who becomes a besom-maker).

Because of their association with witchcraft, besoms continued to play a potent part in literature and films. *Fantasia*, for example, the animated Disney film from 1940, has a particularly scary scene—called "The Sorcerer's Apprentice"—in which Mickey Mouse is terrified by a magic besom, while working for a magician called Yen Sid (Disney spelled backward). In the more recent Harry Potter series, magical flying broomsticks are used by players of the game Quidditch. In *Harry Potter and the Goblet of Fire*, Harry trades up his Nimbus 2000 for a Firebolt, which is supposed to be the fastest model in the business, as well as the most expensive racing broom in existence.

In *Quidditch Through the Ages*, J. K. Rowling explains that there are three rules of the game that pertain directly to broomsticks:

- *Blagging*: No player may seize any part of an opponent's broom to slow or hinder the player.
- *Blatching*: No player may fly with the intent to collide.
- *Blurting*: No player may lock broom handles with the intent to steer an opponent off course.

The **BLEED NIPPLE** is the name of the tiny screw that is found at the top end of a radiator and allows the escape of excess air from the system.

It sits inside the **bleed valve** and is turned by the **bleed key**, that specialized spanner (usually made of solid brass) that you can never find around the house when you need it.

The bleed valve is not to be confused with the **manual control valve**, which is the one at the top of the little pipe up from the floor that controls the temperature, or the **lockshield valve**, which is the one at the other end, which has the purpose of keeping the flow of water through the system even.

When new water is added to a central heating system, a certain amount of air goes with it. The action of the pump also adds air. This rises in water and collects at high points, preventing the system from dispensing heat properly. If your radiators feel cool at their top ends, you need to bleed them—as follows.

Turn on the heating to get warm water into your system. Then switch it off again. If you keep the pump on, there's always the risk that new air may be drawn in, making your problems worse. Now fit the bleed key into the bleed valve, turn the key anticlockwise half a turn, and listen as the trapped air hisses out. Eventually the air will all have gone, to be replaced by first a dribble and then a spurt of dirty water—the **bleed water.*** You should wrap a rag around the key to catch this. A sealed system will now need to be repressurized.

If you should ever get into the disastrous situation where a jet of boiling water is shooting unstoppably across the room from the bleed valve, it's highly likely that you have (a) tried to bleed the radiator while the heating was still on, and/or (b) turned the bleed nipple so far in the valve that it has come loose and shot out onto the floor. Your best bet in this situation is to jam a towel as quickly as possible over the leaking valve. Trying not to scald your hands, then push a knob of chewing gum into the bleed valve as a stopgap. Get down on your knees and find the nipple. Replace it, and screw in tight with the bleed key. Then sit down, breathe a sigh of relief, and vow never to bleed the radiators with the heating on ever again.

*If the water is brown or orange, you have serious problems and should consult a plumber immediately.

A **BOBÈCHE** (pronounced *boh-besh*) is the ring at the top of a candlestick, used to catch melted wax running down the side of the candle.

This feature was later copied on electric lights. Chandelier bobèches, made from lead crystal or brass, can be much larger than those that would be required by mere candles, up to twelve inches in diameter.

Chandeliers were first used in medieval times to light churches and large halls. The simplest form was a wooden cross, with spikes to hold candles. Subsequently, larger forms of candleholder were devised, using ring or crown designs, becoming ever more elaborate. By the eighteenth century, brass chandeliers with curved arms holding many candles were widely used.

As lead crystal became cheaper during the eighteenth century, glass chandeliers became more and more popular. Light was scattered and refracted by the many transparent pendants, and chandeliers became beautiful centerpieces, not to mention status symbols. With the introduction of gas and then electricity, the chandelier continued its magnificent progress, carrying over key features of its candle-bearing days, most particularly the bobèche.

A **BOLERO** is a short jacket, usually worn by women. Sleeves may run to the wrist, or be cropped higher up the arm.

Originally worn by matadors in Spain, the bolero is still an essential part of the *traje de luces* or suit of lights, the ceremonial gear worn by the *torero* (bull handler) at a bullfight. The silk jacket is often heavily embroidered in gold and can be the handiwork of up to fifty people, costing thousands of dollars. Beneath are skintight trousers, and on the head a *montera*, or bicorne hat. A matador needs at least six such suits a season.

The bolero was also a key part of a woman's wedding dress in nineteenth-century Turkey, where it was paired with the *salvar* (baggy trousers).

The jazz group Herb Alpert and the Tijuana Brass wore matching bolero jackets in the 1960s and 1970s; the garment found stardom again in the 1990s, when Paul Mercurio wore one in the climactic scene of the Australian hit film *Strictly Ballroom*.

In the world of ballroom dancing, a bolero is not, as a

rule, a jacket but a romantic dance, which originated in Spain in the late eighteenth century and subsequently became popular in Cuba and Latin America. It was further popularized across the world after, in 1928, the French composer Maurice Ravel wrote his ballet score *Bolero* for dancer Ida Rubenstein, which was a huge hit at its American premiere. The catchy one-movement orchestral piece reemerged in the late 1970s in the film *10*, which featured Dudley Moore and Bo Derek as a middle-aged songwriter and a gorgeous young bride (not his), who ended up making love on a beach to the insistent ostinato rhythm. Sales of the music subsequently rocketed worldwide, and were repeated in the mid-1980s following the medal-winning ice-dance performance of English skaters Jayne Torvill and Christopher Dean.

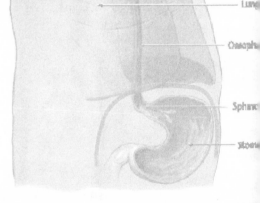

A **BOLUS** is a lump of food, *while* it is actually in your mouth: a soft, soggy, roundish wad of predigested mush, moistened by your saliva, shaped by your tongue, and chewed and ground down by your molars, until it is sufficiently reduced in size to slide down the hatch.

Side view of respiratory and digestive anatomy

BORBORYGMUS (pronounced *bor-buh-rig-mus*) is the name for the rumbling, gurgling, growling sounds made by the stomach.

These are caused by the movement of fluids and gases, as food, acids, and digestive juices migrate from the stomach into the upper part of the small intestine, before heading on down the twenty-foot-long gastrointestinal tract, propelled by a squeezing action known as **peristalsis**.

The average body makes two gallons of digestive juices a day. The hydrochloric acid in your stomach is so strong it could eat into metal, but a special form of mucus protects your inner linings from this acid along the length of its journey.

The **BRANNOCK DEVICE** is that wonderfully old-fashioned-looking measuring instrument, patented in 1926 by Charles F. Brannock of Syracuse, New York, and still found in shoe shops in every mall or Main Street in the land.

All feet, adults' and children's, can be sized by the same three dimensions that the Brannock Device measures: heel-to-toe, arch (heel to ball of foot), and width.

Slipping your size-four foot into that cold metal was an end-of-summer ritual, before going back to school and waiting for the next growth spurt.

A **BURGEE** (pronounced bur-jee) is the little triangular flag that flutters on a sailing dinghy, traditionally at the top of the main mast, but sometimes from a pole on the **bow pulpit** or even in the **starboard rigging**.

As well as giving a useful indication of the direction of the wind, the burgee often proclaims membership of a particular yacht club. An old tradition dictates that if you visit a club not previously visited by a member of your own, you should exchange burgees. Many yacht clubs display their collections of exchanged burgees in a case behind the bar, or even, these days, up on a Web site.

Strict etiquette controls the flying of the burgee, as it does other maritime flags. It may be flown day or night, but never when racing (when a square racing flag is sported).

As anyone who has been out with a keen dinghy sailor knows, the sport of sailing is littered with precise terms for bits of the boat that it's extremely important to get right. This is not an area where you can get away with "that whatchamacallit" unless you want to be thrown overboard by your irate captain, whose sense of humor may only return when he (and it so often is a he) gets back to port and into the bar. A boat is only a boat if it's small; otherwise, it's a **ship**. It does not have a left and right, but a **port** and **starboard**; nor a front or back, but a **bow** and a **stern**. The big sail may be the **mainsail**, but the secondary sail is not the lesser or smaller sail, it's the **jib**. The wooden pole under the mainsail is the **boom**. The front of the sail is the **luff** or **leading edge**. The taut wires that hold things up are **stays**. Ropes are called **halyards**, **sheets**, or **painters**, unless they hold the sail to the boom, in which case they're **tacks**. The contraption out the back that steers the boat is the **tiller**; the **rudder** is only the bit below the water. Those pincerlike whatchamacallits that hold the sheets in place when you're sailing are **cleats**. That bit of wood that drops through a slit in the center of the hull is not "the thing that holds the boat upright" but the **centerboard** or **daggerboard**.

OK? Now all you have to learn are the terms to do with the actual sailing of the lovely craft, which, incidentally, is always a female: you sail in *her* and *she* speeds over the waves.

A **BURPEE** is a calisthenic exercise performed to increase strength and energy; it is named after the American doctor Royal Burpee.

The word calisthenic comes from the Greek *kallos*, beauty, and *sthenos*, strength. The burpee is designed to achieve bodily fitness and grace of movement; when repeated, it also improves cardiovascular fitness.

To perform a burpee, move from a standing position to a squat, before thrusting your legs out behind you, while keeping your upper body at arm's length off the ground. The legs are then brought back into a squat, before you spring back to a standing position. For maximum benefit, the exercise should be done in a fluid, constant movement, without pauses.

Much like the Royal Canadian Air Force exercises, the burpee has an institutional following; its devoted adherents range from athletes who have learned it on circuit training to those who have come across it in the services. It is popular, too, in prisons, where space is limited.

A **CADENZA** is an ornamental passage in a longer piece of music, which allows a soloist to show off his or her skill on an instrument.

The cadenza originated as a vocal flourish in an opera, when a singer would elaborate on a **cadence** in an **aria** (or operatic song). Later it was taken up in instrumental music, and in due course the improvised element was dropped as composers began writing out their own cadenzas.

Third parties also wrote cadenzas for works by other composers. Beethoven, for example, wrote cadenzas for Mozart's Piano Concerto No. 20; Fritz Kreisler wrote cadenzas for Beethoven's Violin Concerto; and Benjamin Britten wrote a cadenza for Haydn's Cello Concerto in C. In a concerto, cadenzas usually occur toward the end of the first movement.

The tradition was taken up in jazz, and is the correct way to describe those bits of the performance where the saxophonist goes off on his own track for a while, to be joined eventually in a funky climax by the rest of the musicians.

The **CALAMUS** is the tubelike part of a bird's feather at its bottom end, where the shaft is hollow and horny, historically known as the **quill**.

When the bird is alive, the word calamus describes the hollow part of the shaft that is embedded in the follicle below the skin. Above the skin, the rest of the shaft, which is not, at that point, hollow, is known as the **rachis**. At the junction of calamus and rachis is a small opening, the **superior umbilicus**, from which often extends a much smaller feather, the **after feather**.

Running outward from the shaft is the **vane** of the feather, consisting of slender filaments known as **barbs**. Attached to these may be further microscopic filaments called **barbules**, which in turn have tiny hooklets, known as **barbicels**, or **hamuli**, which hold the barbules together. When you see a bird grooming or preening itself, it's readjusting the lie of its barbules for best insulation and protection against the wet.

The quill is long forgotten now, superseded

by the steel nib of a pen, then by the tip of the ballpoint and its followers, and finally by the keyboard of the word processor. But from the seventh century right up until the early nineteenth century, when steel nibs first appeared, the quill was the writing instrument of choice. Quills were generally made from goose feathers, with the rarer, more expensive swan quill for the more discerning or prosperous scribe. Crow-feather quills were said to be excellent for drawing fine lines. The feathers of eagles, owls, hawks, and turkeys were also used. Quills were taken from the left wing of a bird, as those feathers curved outward and away from a right-handed writer. Only the five outer wing feathers were considered suitable, usually taken from the bird during its spring period of new feather growth.

To sharpen the quill, a special knife was used—the original **pen knife**.

The **CARUNCULA** is the small, pink protuberance at the corner of the eye.

It is here, after a night's sleep, that a yellowish crust forms, which is a combination of mucus, dust, pollen, and tears—**rheum** is the medical term for it, though it's colloquially known as "sleepy dust" or "sleep."

All these substances gather in the eye throughout the day, too, but the constant blinking of the eyelids effectively wipes the eyes clean of foreign substances; the secretions only form the crust when the eyelids stop blinking, during sleep.

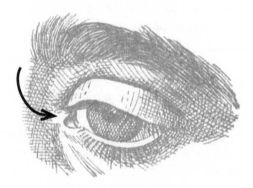

A **CARYATID** is a stone carving of a draped female figure, which in classical architecture takes the place of a column or pillar supporting an **entablature** (the upper external section of a temple).*

The word literally means "woman of Caryae," and one story has it that these stone maidens represent the women of this Peloponnesian town, condemned to slavery because they sided with the Persians during their second invasion of Greece in 480 BC.

The most famous examples are the six figures of the Caryatid porch of the Erechtheum on the Acropolis. Lord Elgin took one of these figures back with him to Britain in the early 1800s; it is now to be found in the British Museum. The other five are in the Acropolis Museum in Athens.

* See **Architrave** (p. 9).

Similar figures, but with baskets on their heads, are called **canephores**; they represent the maidens who carried the sacred objects used at the feasts of the goddesses Athena and Artemis.

Caryatids made a reappearance in building façades in the sixteenth century, and can be seen on such disparate buildings as St. Pancras New Church in London, the Austrian Parliament in Vienna, and the Museum of Science and Industry in Chicago. The male equivalent is called an **Atlas**; more than one of these sturdy stone fellers are known as **Atlantes**.

The **CHEONGSAM** (pronounced *chong-sam*) is a silk dress of southern Chinese origin, with a slit skirt and high mandarin collar.

Known in China as the *qipao*, it dates from the Empire of the Great Qing (1644–1911), China's last ruling dynasty. Though the original garment was much looser than the modern version, the rulers of this dynasty were from Manchuria, and required men and women to wear Manchu clothes—the *qipao* included—on pain of death.

The elegant body-hugging garment of today is worn by flight attendants on some Chinese airlines—and by receptionists in Chinese restaurants the world over. After the actress Nancy Kwan wore one in the 1960 film *The World of Suzie Wong*, the cheongsam became fashionable in the West, and is currently favored by heiress and fashion plate Paris Hilton.

A **CLAQUE** is a group of people in a theater or opera audience, who are hired by a performer or producer to applaud a performance.

So the euphoric reception that sometimes greets the great baritone or tenor may, in fact, have been supercharged by injections of . . . cash (or at least a free ticket). Sometimes, rival performers will have each hired a claque, and then the competing applause is as entertaining as the arias in the piece.

Claques are no new phenomenon, dating back to the comedy competitions of ancient Athens, where contestants' chances were boosted by groups of paid supporters. Claques were common in the theaters of the Roman Empire; the Emperor Nero paid a claque of five thousand soldiers to follow him on his concert tours and even established a school of applause. The theaters of nineteenth-century France were famous for their claques, which were divided into those who laughed loudly at comedies (*rieurs*), those who cried pitifully during the moving moments of tragedies (*pleureuses*), and those who called for encores at the end of a performance (*bisseurs*).

Claques continue, though mainly now in the world of opera. Milan's La Scala has a famous claque, which includes teachers, students of music, and, allegedly, two barbers; the directors of the claque get a small fee, while the rest are content with free admission.

Studio audiences for TV shows don't even need a claque. Applauding loudly in response to held-up cards, they are all claquers, happy to support the performers in return for a free ticket.

A **CLERIHEW** is a gently satirical, biographical, four-line verse, rhymed as two couplets, often with lines of uneven length.

It is named after its inventor, the writer Edmund Clerihew Bentley (1875–1956), who started composing these verses as a boy, when he was bored in the classroom. He persuaded his friend G. K. Chesterton to write some as well.

Here is one of Bentley's original clerihews from his school period:

*Sir Humphry Davy**
Abominated gravy.
He lived in the odium
Of having discovered sodium.

⁓⁓⁓

*Whether the distinguished British scientist Sir Humphry Davy (1778–1829) really disliked gravy is not known. But the second half of the couplet certainly has some truth in it. After the Italian scientist Alessandro Volta invented the first battery in 1800, Davy used it to isolate sodium and potassium for the first time, and later strontium,

Here's another:

The people of Spain think Cervantes
Equal to half a dozen Dantes;
An opinion resented most bitterly
By the people of Italy.

barium, and magnesium, opening up the field of electrochemistry. In 1815, after receiving a letter from some Newcastle miners, which told of the dangers they faced from methane gas underground, he invented the Davy lamp, which became widely used.

A **CONTRAIL** is the long, thin trail left behind by an airplane when it's flying high enough for the cold to turn the exhaust vapor into ice crystals. Indeed, a **condensation trail** (to give it its full name) is, in effect, a very long, thin, man-made cloud.

On rare occasions, you may observe the inverse of a contrail, a **dissipation trail**, where the jet's exhaust appears to cut a slash of clear sky through an already existing cloud. These **distrails** are formed by various effects of the exhaust on the ice particles that make up the cloud.

Contrails may look like big swathes of pollution in the sky, but though they contain hydrocarbons, sulphates, nitrogen, carbon dioxide, and water vapor, they produce, comparatively, far less "greenhouse gas" than motor vehicles or power plants. Modern aircraft engines, which have been designed to burn fuel more efficiently and emit less carbon dioxide, actually create more contrails than their predecessors.

Scientists are still studying the extent to which contrails affect global warming in other ways. It seems clear that, en masse, they create a thin blanket of cloud high up at the top of the troposphere, which has a heat-trapping effect. But it is also true that the highly reflective particles contained in contrails turn back the sun's rays, leading to a global heat reduction.

In the three days after September 11, 2001, when all commercial flights over the United States were banned, there were no contrails in American skies, and the difference between daytime and nighttime temperatures was found to be 1.1°C greater than normal. The conclusion some meteorologists drew from this was that contrails reduce ground temperatures during the day and increase them at night, which bears out both effects described above. But the jury is still out on their total contribution to global warming.

Contrails would vanish from our skies overnight if jet aircraft were banned from traveling at high altitude. However, flying lower, aircraft would need more fuel to get through the denser air, with an estimated increase in carbon-dioxide emissions of 4 percent.

One particular group is agreed on the deleterious effect of contrails. Albeit thin, the layer of cloud they create completely spoils the clear skies required by astronomers with land-based telescopes.

The **CRADLE SWITCH** is that part of the telephone on which the receiver-cum-mouthpiece rests.

Even the most contemporary of landline telephones maintain this feature, though cell phones have dispensed with it entirely. Remember: if you put the receiver down on an outgoing call, the call will be disconnected; on an incoming call, however, the line remains connected until the caller hangs up.

Alexander Graham Bell (1847–1922), the inventor of the telephone, was born into a Scottish family with an enthusiastic interest in communication. His grandfather, Alexander Bell, had been an actor and orator who worked to help people with speech impediments and was nicknamed the "Professor of Elocution" by the press of his day; his two sons, David and Melville, followed in his footsteps, becoming elocutionists and speech teachers. Ironically, when Melville married, it was to a deaf woman, Eliza Grace Symonds. Hardly surprisingly, he subsequently became fascinated with ways of communicating with the deaf, developing a system he called Visible Speech Techniques.

As their son, young Alexander, grew up, he attempted to communicate with his mother in his own way: by speaking in a low, deep voice close to her forehead. He was a curious and inventive child. On a visit to London, as a teenager, he saw a "speaking machine" in operation. Inspired, he worked with his brother to develop his own machine, which resembled a human mouth—and which made speechlike sounds. He continued to study the characteristics and patterns of sound, believing that he might eventually find a way to transmit sound electrically. After a bout of tuberculosis killed both his brothers, Bell moved to the United States, eventually teaching Visible Speech at the Boston School for Deaf Mutes (where he met and married one of his pupils).

Samuel Morse's development of telegraphy in the 1840s had revolutionized communication, but hand-delivery was still required between the telegraph station and the recipient. Bell remained convinced that sound waves, and thus, ultimately, the human voice, could travel along wires, and he began work on something he called a "harmonic telegraph."

He formed a partnership with Thomas Watson, a scientist who also believed that speech might be transmitted electrically. On March 10, 1876, while they were working on their project in separate rooms, Bell spilled some battery acid over his jacket, and shouted out, "Mr. Watson, come here. I want you." A revolutionary moment had arrived. Watson heard Bell's voice through the wire—and became the first person in the world to receive a telephone call.

Bell and Watson were able to patent their invention, and became rich. But Bell was never interested in the mere business of telephones, devoting himself instead to other areas of scientific innovation. He contributed to aviation technology and developed a precursor to modern-day air-conditioning in his own home, among other achievements. His last patent, at the age of seventy-five, was for a rapid hydrofoil.

Bell remained committed to the advancement of science and technology. In 1898 he took over the presidency of a small, almost unheard-of scientific society: the National Geographic Society. Bell and his son-in-law, Gilbert Grosvenor, added beautiful photographs and interesting writing to what had been a fairly dry publication—turning *National Geographic* into one of the world's best-known magazines.

Alexander Graham Bell died on August 2, 1922. On the day of his burial, all telephone service in the United States was stopped for one minute in his honor.

The **CRASH BAR** is the metal bar mounted horizontally across the exit door, which you often find at the bottom of echoing stone staircases in unmodernized theaters and cinemas.

When you push down on the bar, the attached lever forces a latch bolt to rotate and disengage from the **door strike** (the metal plate on the side of the door—or **jamb**—into which the latch fits when the door is closed).

Crash bars may have a retro look, but modern fire codes in countries the world over require them on all fire and emergency exits.

One of the earliest law codes was the Code of Hammurabi, created in 1760 BC by the Babylonian king of that name. A number of the 282 laws in this code dealt with penalties for shoddy building practices: in particular, if a builder didn't construct a house properly and it collapsed and killed his client, the builder too should be put to death; if the house fell over and killed the son of his client, the son of the builder should be put to death; if it killed one or more of the owner's slaves, the builder was obliged to recompense him, slave for slave.

A **CROUSTADE** is a molded or hollowed-out crust, used as an edible serving container for a tasty filling.

Usually made from puff or flaky pastry, croustades may also be fashioned from bread, potato, rice, semolina, vermicelli, or even, in an unusual vegetarian version, chestnuts and pumpkin seeds.

Mini-croustades, filled with such delights as peppered goat's cheese, sun-dried tomatoes, seared sea bass, or crawfish tails, are a staple of contemporary canapé menus, alongside many other mini versions of well-known dishes: kebabs, quiches, roulades, and samosas.

Intriguingly, the word canapé derives from *konops*, the Greek for mosquito. From that came *konopeion*, which described an early form of mosquito net, hung over beds. Later the word was assimilated into Old French, where it came to refer to pieces of furniture that incorporated curtains, such as four-poster beds. French chefs took the word from there, to describe a pastry or bread appetizer covered, canopylike, with a savory topping.

In the 1970s, when you could still find shrimp cocktail served as an appetizer in neighborhood bistros, such a thing as a mini-croustade would have been unheard of. At that time, the trendsetting hostess's party dishes were full of such delicious tidbits as sausage rolls, vol-au-vents, cubes of cheese with pickled onions or wedges of pineapple, and, of course, the *canapé de résistance*—the devil-on-horseback, a prune (sometimes stuffed with cream cheese) wrapped in bacon. Inevitably, fashions moved on. At the smart, yuppie gatherings of the 1980s, the finger food grew ever more adventurous. Continental treats such as quail's eggs, crostini, and bruschette made way in the 1990s for Eastern exotica: Thai fishcakes and chicken satay, Chinese spring rolls, Japanese sushi and nori rolls. As the new century dawned, and the search for novelty grew ever more pressing, mini versions of traditional old favorites began to make an appearance: miniature hamburgers or sliders, caramelized onion tartlets, and, of course, croustades, cut down and redefined with splendid new fillings.

A **CROZIER** is the long stick—or pastoral staff—carried by a bishop dressed up in full **vestments** in order to preside at liturgies or confer sacraments. He* bears this to symbolize that he is a shepherd of God's flock.

The traditional curved or hooked top echoes the design of a shepherd's crook and is intended to draw back those who stray, while the pointed **ferrule** at the bottom is there to goad the spiritually lazy. When the bishop is inside his diocese, the staff

*In the United Kingdom, bishops are all still male, though since July 8, 2008, the Anglican Church has officially accepted the possibility of female bishops. In the United States, the Episcopal Church elected Katharine Jefferts Schori as presiding bishop in June 2006.

is held with its curve facing out; when outside, the curve faces in.

Despite its ancient appearance and powerful symbolism, the crozier does not date back to the earliest days of Christianity—it was first used in the Middle Ages. Initially, it seems to have been just a straight staff, but a basic bent crook was soon added, which was later combined with designs and figures (snakes' and dragons' heads were popular).

The naming of the rest of the bishop's formal apparel offers a challenge to all but the most dedicated of worshippers. Starting from the top, the triangular-shaped hat is the **mitre**. The band around the neck is the **amice apparel**, and the little scarflike bit of cloth that flops down onto the left shoulder is the **lappet**. Below that, the long triangular-bottomed outer wrap is the **chasuble**, decorated on the chest with the highly embroidered band, often of gold, that is the **orphrey**. The scarf that hangs from the left hand is the **maniple**.

On the lower part of the body, below the chasuble, are three layers. The petticoatlike **alb** is covered with the **tunicle**, over which hangs the wide-sleeved, loose **dalmatic**. Between the alb and the tunicle hangs the long scarf that is the **stole**.

Below all this, on his feet, the bishop wears **sanctuary slippers**. On his hands he may wear gloves, beneath which will be the **episcopal ring**.

Unlike the parvenu crozier, most of this splendid array of garments can be traced back to the earliest days of the Church. The alb is very similar to the light tunic customarily worn by clergy in those times; the stole is developed from the scarf commonly worn around the neck by the Romans; the chasuble relates back to a simple mantle worn by working people; and the dalmatic was worn by the upper classes in Dalmatia.

Much of this clothing is also symbolic: the alb stands for purity and innocence; the stole for patience; and the maniple for strength and endurance.

CUMULONIMBUS is the name for that mighty, rain-bearing cloud that resembles a sky-borne mountainous landscape.

Such a cloud can tower up from just above ground level to heights of 45,000 feet, its dark top spreading out into the freezing upper troposphere as the anvil-shaped **incus** (known colloquially as the anvil head). As it masses up on a sunny summer's afternoon, you know that it's time to pack away the beach towels and head for home; this monster signals rain, if not a drenching thunderstorm.

The names for all the main cloud forms come from combinations of five Latin words: *cirrus*, meaning a curl of hair; *cumulus*, a heap; *stratus*, a layer; *altus*, high; and *nimbus*, a raincloud. These terms were first suggested in 1802 by the amateur English meteorologist Luke Howard, in a paper to the Askesian Society (a debating club for scientific thinkers, which lasted from 1796 to 1807). **Cirrus** clouds are found at the highest levels, above 23,000 feet, where temperatures are so low that the clouds are made up of ice crystals. Like the hair they were named after, cirrus clouds often come in isolated tufts, thin filaments, or threads spreading out into featherlike forms. **Cirrostratus**, on the other hand, is a thin, whitish sheet of cloud, sometimes covering

the sky completely, often forming a glowing halo around sun or moon. **Cirrocumulus** describes the third kind of high cloud: the beautiful masses of tiny, globular cloudlets sometimes called a mackerel sky. Between 23,000 feet and 7,000 feet are found intermediate-level clouds with the alto prefix: **altocumulus** clouds may be arranged in groups or lines, often so closely packed that their edges are confused; blue sky can generally be seen behind. **Altostratus**, by contrast, forms a thick, gray or bluish-colored sheet (when it displays a rippling effect, it is known as **altostratus undulatus**).

Lower clouds are found below 7,000 feet. The correct name for the famous "cotton-wool" cloud is **fair-weather cumulus,** so called because it presages a fine day of sunny spells. When the weather starts to turn, the sky fills with the large masses or rolls of cloud known as **stratocumulus**, leaving just the odd patch of blue here and there. These may then be replaced by the mighty cumulonimbus.

The dreary, gray, rain-bearing sheet of cloud that can

make a total misery of a day out is **nimbostratus**. This can reach from as low as 1,000 feet up to 20,000 feet. It is not, however, to be confused with the lowest cloud of all, the gray, featureless, but generally dry **stratus**, which may reach right down to the ground and also be called **fog**.

The type of cloud formation present gives an indication of the sort of weather to be expected:

- Cirrus—unsettled weather coming
- Cirrostratus—showers or rain soon
- Cirrocumulus—unsettled weather
- Altocumulus—sunny periods
- Altostratus—rain likely
- Fair-weather cumulus—sunny spells
- Stratocumulus—dry but dull weather
- Cumulonimbus—heavy rain or thunderstorm in the offing
- Nimbostratus—in fact, it's raining now

"Clouds are subject to certain distinct modifications, produced by the general causes which affect all the variations of the atmosphere; they are commonly as good visible indicators of the operation of these causes as is the countenance of the state of a person's mind or body."

Luke Howard, 1802, in a paper to the
Askesian Society

The **CUTWATER** is the triangular stone part of a multiple-arch bridge, between the arches, that breaks (or cuts) the water flowing past.

The arches themselves are mounted on the **piers** of the bridge, which are hidden beneath the water. The point at which the piers meet the arches, around the water-level, is called the **springing**. At each end of the bridge you find the **abutment**, which restrains the horizontal thrust of the bridge and its load.

The width of each arch is described as its **span**; the height as its **rise**; and the relation between these two measurements is known as the **span-to-rise ratio**. Florence's

famous Ponte Vecchio, which was built in 1345 after the destruction by flood of its wooden predecessor, is an early example of a high span-to-rise ratio, namely 5:1. Arch bridges were first used by the Romans, though the stone arch itself was a feature of the Indus Valley civilization of 2500 BC.

The **DAP** is the name for the touching, or bumping, of fists between friends as a greeting or to celebrate victory.

Originally exclusive to the African-American community, the gesture reached national—and international—prominence on June 3, 2008, when Barack Obama bumped fists with his wife, Michelle, before announcing his historic nomination as the Democratic Party's first nonwhite candidate for the presidency.

Known also as power five, fist bump, and quarter pounder, the dap was originally an acronym for Dignity and Pride and has been around for at least as long as Obama himself. It was used on TV in the 1970s by NBA players, such as Baltimore Bullets guard Fred Carter. In the 1980s, it was exchanged between two of the characters in Winona Ryder's angsty teenage movie *Heathers*.

Now it's reached the super-mainstream, it may well go the way of other celebrated gestures and catchphrases from the black community, such as the high five and Wassup—more used by whites trying to be hip than anyone else.

The **DECKLE** is that little extra bit of fat that comes with the **point cut** of a **brisket**.

The point cut is harder to find than the more common **flat cut**, which is both leaner and thinner. However, the fat from the deckle greatly improves the flavor of the brisket, if allowed to soak into the meat during cooking.

The brisket itself is the cut of meat that comes from the breast or lower chest of an animal, beneath the first five ribs, behind the **foreshank**. Though all meat animals have a brisket, the term is usually applied to beef or veal. One of the tougher cuts of meat, the brisket needs long and slow cooking to break down the collagen in the connective muscle tissues found in this section of the animal. The meat is often used, chopped, in a pot roast or casserole, or else marinated or smoked. The brisket is a staple of Jewish cooking, often served sliced as an entrée, particularly on religious holidays. Sweet brisket is served at Rosh Hashanah (Jewish New Year) for a sweet new year.

The brisket is one of the eight beef **primal cuts**. The others being, from front to back: **chuck**, **rib**, **short loin**, **sirloin**, **round**, then below, **brisket**, **short plate**, and **flank**.

The rib cuts provide spare ribs and rib-eye steaks. Short loin becomes T-bone and Porterhouse. Sirloin and rump are the tenderest and most prized, lending their names to those steaks on the table.

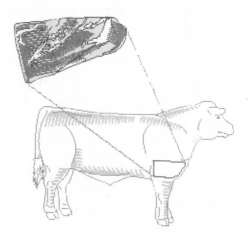

A **DEELEY-BOBBER** is a wacky party accessory that makes the wearer look like an alien.

A hair band, two glitter balls or furry ears, perched upon springy "antlers"—*et voilà*!

Nothing says party (like it's 1982) more than this wonderful piece of festive gear. In the Deeley-bobber's heyday, no self-respecting fun-lover, male or female, would hit the party without one.

Said to have originated from John Belushi's "Killer Bees" skit on *Saturday Night Live*, Deeley-bobbers became popular at a time when aliens were all the rage (and the electronic

game of Space Invaders was to be found in every bar in the land). When registering its trademark name in 1982, Ace Novelty Company called it "a headband with springs carrying ornaments."

The Deeley-bobber is less often seen now, though still a popular accessory at children's parties and girls' nights out.

A **DESICCANT BAG** is one of those bags full of powder you often find accompanying newly bought goods, from computers to clothes to handbags.

Its purpose is to bring on or maintain a state of dryness in a product that might be sensitive to moisture or humidity. Two of the most common desiccants are silica gel and calcium chloride. Sometimes you may see more primitive, old-fashioned desiccants, such as grains of rice in salt shakers.

Double-glazed windows also make use of dessicants, which are placed inside the spacer bar between the two panes of a unit to dry out any trapped moisture.

The **DESIRE LINE** is the path that people most want to take, and will take—no matter where an existing track, pavement, or road may lead.

You can see the desire line, straight or slightly crooked, beaten across muddy fields or grassy hillsides, avoiding the carefully signed route the authorities would prefer you to use.

The **DEWCLAW** is the tiny fifth claw on the inner part of a dog's leg above the other toes, so called, rather romantically, because it brushes the dew from the grass. Dogs almost always have these tiny talons on the inside of their front legs and sometimes also on their hind legs.

Some owners and vets say that dewclaws are useless, and should be removed, as they can get torn or cause damage (to clothes, furniture, and the like). Others claim that this odd appendage is very useful to a dog: to help pick up bones and sticks; for grip in hunting and climbing; to scratch an itch; even to remove objects stuck in their teeth.

The dewclaw on the front leg is sometimes also described as a **first digit**; in this case, the word dewclaw is used to describe the **vestigial claw** on the rear leg, which is higher up, has no muscular control and, it seems, no purpose.

A number of mountain

shepherding breeds—the Saint Bernard, Pyrenean mastiff, and so on—have been selectively bred for **polydactyly**—having multiple digits that are often mobile and controllable. To meet the breed standards recognized by international kennel clubs, dogs must have their fore and/or hind dewclaws intact. Indeed, some double-dewclawed dogs will be favored over single-clawed equivalents. Many French Beauceron breeders, for example, believe that a dog is not a Beauceron unless it has hind double dewclaws; these enable it to climb onto sheep when herding, as well as helping it move swiftly through snow. The Norwegian Lundehund, likewise, uses its multiple dewclaws to scale cliffs and hunt puffins.

There are many other specialized terms for the body parts of man's best friend, which anyone wanting to join in those doggy conversations in the park should master. Most would know the **tail**, **muzzle**, and possibly the **hock**, which is the correct word for the joint between the knee and the foot. But how many non-petlovers could place the **croup**, the **withers**, and the **pastern**? Those jowly flaps of loose skin around the neck are **dewlaps**; and that red membrane inside the lower eyelid, which you may notice as a dog looks balefully at you while you're eating, is the **haw**.

There are almost 250 breeds of dog and these are split into seven groups,* according to their proportions and

⌒⌒⌒⌒

*The American Kennel Club recognizes 148 breeds, the Kennel Club UK 209; both have seven groups, although some terms differ.

characteristics: **terrier**, **working**, **sporting**, **hound**, **herding**, **toy**, and **nonsporting**.

- Terriers have been bred to flush out prey such as foxes, badgers, and rabbits, so are consequently small, to fit into tunnels. They are much more aggressive than their size might suggest. Some breeds are wire-haired to give them extra protection (e.g., Airedale, Norfolk, and Scottish terriers).
- Working dogs have been bred to herd livestock, pull sledges, search and rescue, guard, or even identify items such as drugs; they are generally even-tempered, energetic, easy to train, and obedient (e.g., boxer, Great Dane, Saint Bernard).
- Sporting dogs are bred with exaggerated instincts and need little training to point or retrieve. **Pointers** (as their name suggests) will spot game and silently point to its whereabouts with raised nose and forepaw, while **retrievers** will retrieve shot game without damage (e.g., Irish setter, golden retriever, English cocker spaniel).
- Hounds have been bred for hunting and tracking. They have an acute sense of smell and will bay when on the trail of a prey. They are renowned for their stamina (e.g., beagle, whippet, greyhound).
- Toy dogs are bred for domestic use. They are small and sociable, so are suitable for confined living spaces. Many of the dogs you see trotting around the park after fashionably dressed people in cities are toy dogs (e.g., King Charles spaniel, Pekingese).

- Nonsporting dogs include medium to large purebreds that differ in conformation and characteristics. Some of the oldest documented breeds in the world fall into this category (e.g., bulldog, Dalmatian, poodle).

A **DIBBLE** (or dibber) is a pointed gardening instrument used to make holes in the ground, generally for planting bulbs or pricking out seedlings. To dibble is to use such a tool.

When using your dibble to plant bulbs, remember that they should be put in at a depth at least two to three times their height and two bulb widths apart. When the soil is replaced on top, there should be no air spaces around the bulbs. Spring bulbs should ideally be planted by the end of September, and certainly well before the first frosts set in.

A **DONGLE** is a small **hardware device** that plugs into a computer, generally to authenticate a particular piece of **software**.

Without the dongle, the software will not run properly, so it can be used as protection against unlicensed copying by unscrupulous users. Generally, dongles are attached to expensive, specialized packages such as translation memory or printing software. The dongle may be encoded with a license key, specific to a particular user, which enables only certain features in the application.

The word dongle can also refer to a laptop Ethernet card adaptor. In many places, too, the word has now become general, referring to other computer **plug-ins**, such as those that enable Bluetooth, or USB modems that allow you, for a fee, to access broadband from anywhere with mobile reception.

DRAGÉES (pronounced *drah-zhay*) are what discriminating children demand on their birthday cakes.

Otherwise known as "those little silver balls," they're smaller than a cultured pearl, made of sugar, and covered with a metallic coating to resemble a ball bearing. Generally, they are as tough to crunch through as a real ball bearing. You can also get them with gold and copper finishes.

Sugared almonds are also called dragées. In France and Italy, these are served at wedding parties—traditionally, *thrown* at the newlywed couple—a custom that is supposed to ensure fertility and lifelong prosperity.

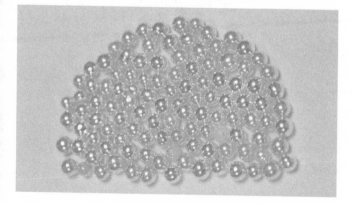

A **DREDGER** is a container
with a perforated lid, which is used for
coating food with powder, such as icing,
sugar, or cinnamon.

You will see a dredger full of chocolate powder to sprinkle over your cappuccino at your local coffee shop.

DRUPELETS are the little globules that make up a raspberry or blackberry.

Though both fruits are from the same family, raspberry drupelets are hairy and blackberry drupelets are smooth. All the drupelets are attached to the central core of the fruit, which is called the **receptacle**.

One of the most intriguing things about the raspberry is the word itself—with its curious silent "p" (also found in cupboard and psychiatrist). "C" can be silent too—as in blancmange and Connecticut— and gnus and gnats will tell you on no account to pronounce the "g"—otherwise they might gnash their teeth at you.

The **ESCUTCHEON** is the back plate around a light switch, a door handle, or a keyhole.

Escutcheons are both ornamental, in that they draw the eye to the keyhole, and protective, because they safeguard a door's woodwork from marks made by fumbling key-holders, or smudges of dirty fingers around light switches.

Another important item of door furniture is the **finger-plate**. Again, it protects a door from the accumulation of dirt left by people pushing it open with their hands. It is usually positioned at chest height opposite the hinge, which is the natural place to push a door.

An **EYE** is the name given to any one of the holes in the popular Swiss cheese called Emmental.

The best of this tasty hard cheese, much used in sandwiches and for cheese on toast, is called Emmentaler Swiss. Under European law, only cheese made in the Emme valley outside Berne, and by a particular process, may qualify for this label; like a fine wine, it has an Appellation of Controlled Origin.

The milk used to make Emmentaler Swiss should strictly come from pasture-fed cows. When the milk is heated, and various bacteria introduced, bubbles of carbon dioxide form, which produce the holes. Traditionally, the eyes must be between the size of a twenty-centime piece, at 21 mm roughly the size of a cherry, and a two-franc piece, which is 27.5 mm across, about the size of a large hazelnut.

There is currently controversy in the cheese world, because the U.S. Department of Agriculture is demanding that the eyes become smaller. This is because American slicing machines are unable to cut cheese with large eyes into thin slices without it crumbling. So the Swiss have been instructed that the eyes must measure between a third to three-quarters of an inch in diameter. The Swiss don't like to be told how to make their cheese, and certainly not by a nation whose most famous contribution to the art of cheesemaking is Philadelphia cream cheese.

The **F-HOLE** is a long, narrow hole in the **soundboard** (or top surface) of a violin; shaped like an old-fashioned "f"—or "s" to modern eyes—each instrument has two: one to each side of the **bridge**, at the delicate central curve of the **waist**.

The purpose of the f-hole is not merely decorative: it helps the violin project its sound more efficiently; not so much because it is a hole but because it lets the sounding board vibrate more strongly.

On other acoustic stringed instruments, similar sound-holes have different shapes: guitars have circles, lutes have rosettes.

The violin in its present form emerged in the sixteenth century in northern Italy, most likely a descendant of the two-stringed Arabic **rabab** and similar fiddles of Central Asia. The first violin documented as having four strings was made in 1555 by Andrea Amati of Cremona. Over the next century, the instrument gained popularity—by 1660 the French king Charles IX had ordered twenty-four. The Amati family continued to be known for their violin-making. Andrea was succeeded by Antonio, Hieronymus, Nicolo, and Hieronymus II. Other celebrated families of **luthiers** were the Guarneri, the Stradivari, and the Gagliani. Instruments made by these craftsmen continue to be highly sought-after, by collectors and performers alike. In May 2006, a violin made by Antonio Stradivari* (c. 1644–1737), known as "The Hammer," was sold at Christie's auction house for the record sum of $3,544,000.

*Stradivarius is the Latinized version of his name.

A **FASCINATOR** is a decorative headpiece attached to the hair with a comb, clip, or headband.

Fashioned from beads, crystals, feathers, flowers, sinamay, taffeta, and sometimes even straw, the fascinator offers a chance for the wearer to be stylish and entirely original. It's also ideal for women who don't want to go the whole hog and wear a hat at a formal occasion, be that a wedding, a christening, a race day, or a black-tie event. Some fascinators even have partial veils attached, so they can be worn at funerals.

FINES are the dusty remnants at the bottom of cereal boxes—particularly delicious in the more sugary brands.

However, now that sweetened cereals have been identified as major contributors to children's obesity, manufacturers are decreasing the amount of sugar added. (Until quite recently, many cereal brands contained over 55 percent sugar.)

The cold cereal business began in the late nineteenth century with the search for a healthier diet, and as an alternative to the heavy, meat-laden breakfasts people were eating at the time, which were causing a variety of gastrointestinal disorders. In 1863, James Caleb Jackson developed the first breakfast cereal, which he called Granula. It was a healthy concoction of grains, nuts, and husks of bran. Unfortunately, Granula had to be soaked in cold water at least overnight, and even then it had a rough, tough consistency, felt heavy in the stomach, and, by all accounts, didn't taste very nice. It was not a commercial success.

Thirty years later, the production of corn flakes began by accident. In 1894, Dr. John Harvey Kellogg, and his brother Will, who ran a health spa/sanitarium in Battle Creek, Michigan, were experimenting with new recipes for the vegetarian diet they fed their patients. One evening they left some cooked wheat to rest and, when they returned some time later, found it had gone stale. They decided not to waste it by throwing it away but to process it by pressing it between rollers. They expected to see flat sheets of dough, but instead found flakes, which they toasted and served to their patients, with milk. A year later, they filed a patent for "Flaked Cereals and Process of Preparing Same," which was issued on April 14, 1896, under the name Granose. These eventually became Kellogg's Corn Flakes. After three years, they had sold 1 million boxes.

A **FONTANELLE** is a patch of soft membrane on a baby's head, which has not yet developed into bone; if you look closely, you can see it pulsating.

Though the **anterior** fontanelle at the front is the largest and most visible, a baby has several fontanelles. The next most obvious is the **posterior**—or **occipital**—fontanelle, which is found at the back of the skull, where the **parietal bones** join the **occipital bone**. A more scrupulous study will also reveal the **mastoid** and **sphenoidal** fontanelles.

During birth, the fontanelles allow the skull's bones to flex, enabling the infant's head to pass through the narrow birth canal. As the child grows, the skull hardens, and after several months, the posterior fontanelle will usually be closed over. The anterior fontanelle takes longer, remaining open until the child is almost two.

The range of medical tests run on a small baby includes the **palpation** of the anterior fontanelle: if it's sunken, it may indicate dehydration, while a bulging fontanelle may indicate raised **intracranial pressure**.

Fontanelles seem soft and all too easy to damage. But be reassured: the covering membrane is much tougher than it looks.

The **FROG** is the builder's term for the hollow in the top of a building brick which holds the mortar.

There are several stories about why this indentation is called after a small, tailless amphibian, but the best and simplest explanation is that the name comes from the **block**, or **former**, that is placed in the mold when the brick is made—also called a frog. This was originally made of wood, and, when wet and covered with clay, was supposed to resemble a crouching frog.

Another, more colorful tale traces the name back to the ancient Egyptians, who made hollows in the bricks they manufactured of Nile clay, in which they buried live animals as building work progressed. In 1903, millions of skeletons of *Bufo regularis*, the common African frog, were found in the remains of buildings from ancient Egypt on the Giza Plateau.

A GAFF is a hooked pole traditionally used by fishermen for pulling big fish ashore (or aboard ship).

Once in the fisherman's hands, if the fish is to die, it may well be subjected to a blow from the **priest**, the weighted club that is bashed on the fish's head to finish it off.

If, on the other hand, the fish is to live, a **gag** may come in useful, this being the instrument that holds open the fish's jaws while the hook is removed. Subsequently, the fish may be weighed and thrown back, or held in a **seine net**, which hangs upright in the water.

The use of the gaff is now prohibited in many places for fish intended to be released. It is illegal in the UK.

A **GAMBREL** is a symmetrical, two-sided roof with two slopes on each side, the upper one shallow, the lower one steep.

The idea behind the gambrel is to provide the maximum headspace in the interior of the upper story, while also having the advantages of a sloped roof. It is not to be confused with the **gabled** roof, an ordinary two-sided roof with triangular sections of wall—or gables—at each end. If a roof has four sides, it is called a **hip roof**, and if it has four sides with a gambrel-like double slope, it is called a **mansard**.

The long strips of metal or other strong, weatherproof material, which cover the joints and angles of a roof are called **flashing**; this is not to be confused with **flaunching**, which is the mortar base that holds the chimney pot in position on top of the chimney stack.

GARI is the pink pickled ginger
that is served with sushi.

Its proper purpose is to cleanse the palate between
mouthfuls. It also aids digestion. Though it should really be
eaten a slice at a time, many Western sushi lovers like to
mash it up with the pungent, bright green **wasabi** paste,
which is made from green Japanese horseradish and is there
to enhance the flavor of the sushi.

The word sushi is often used in the West for the generic

dish of raw fish, but, strictly speaking, it describes the cooked rice, delicately flavored with vinegar, which can be topped with vegetables, raw or cooked fish, egg, or even raw meat. The raw fish is called **sashimi** and can be served in bite-sized chunks on its own. Thin slices of raw pheasant and duck have historically also been used for sashimi. Crab, shrimp, octopus, and eel, by contrast, are generally cooked or marinated before being incorporated into sushi.

There are two main types of sushi—**maki** and **nigiri**. Maki is the familiar sushi roll, where the rice and fish are laid on a sheet of dried seaweed—or **nori**—then rolled up, and sliced into loglike sections. Nigiri sushi has one ingredient, such as a slice of raw salmon, sitting on top of an oblong finger of vinegared rice. A form of maki, also known as a **handroll**, is **temaki**, where the fish and rice come in a cone of nori.

Soy sauce—or **shōyu**—is also often served on the side. This is made from fermented soybeans, wheat, and salt, and comes in both light and dark varieties. Dark soy sauce is thicker than light and not as salty. An even darker condiment called **tamari** is wheat-free and more fragrant than soy sauce.

When flavoring nigiri sushi with soy, you should dip only the top, fishy side into the sauce; if you try dipping the rice side, you will find it crumbling into an undignified mess.

In Japan, master sushi chefs undergo a prolonged apprenticeship. Starting in his teens, a typical trainee may spend years just watching his master as he selects the freshest fish in the market. Back in the sushi shop, his jobs will include cleaning, washing up, and delivering sushi around town; he is unlikely to be let near the actual sushi preparation at this stage. Eventually, he will be allowed to watch his master prepare the delicately flavored rice; then to fan the rice to cool it. Only after ten years or so will he be allowed up to the counter at the front of the shop, as an assistant or *wakiita* (literally, side chopping board). Now he will be allowed to roll sushi and prepare fish for more senior chefs. If he proves himself in this role, he will eventually become an *itamae* (literally, in front of the chopping board), allowed to prepare his own sushi for chosen customers.

A **GASKET** is a ring of rubber, asbestos, or metal (among other materials), which is shaped to seal the junction between metal surfaces.

In a car engine, the **head gasket** is crucial in ensuring a good seal between the **cylinder head** and the **cylinder**. If your car "blows a gasket," the seal is broken and you are in serious trouble . . .

Even though most people drive a car regularly, and could easily distinguish between a Porsche and a Dodge, how many of us have even the faintest idea of the difference between the **cams** and the **crankshaft**, let alone what a **tuned port fuel-injection** might be? But, in fact, what lies beneath the **bonnet** of a car is relatively straightforward, and the basic elements of the **internal combustion engine** and its parts can be understood in not much more time than it takes to reverse a car into a tight spot in town.

The internal combustion engine, as its name suggests, is an engine that burns fuel inside itself.* It converts gas into motion by harnessing the energy from hundreds of tiny

---

*In contrast to the **external combustion engine**, such as might be seen on a steam train, which burns fuel outside itself.

explosions per minute, each one of which forces the **piston** down the **cylinder**, turning the **crankshaft**, which, in turn, drives the car. Most engines are powered by more than one cylinder, hence terms such as **four-cylinder**, **eight-cylinder**, and so on.

Each explosion begins with a drop of fuel let in through the **intake valve** at the top of the engine. This then mixes with air before being compressed by the upward motion of the piston. The resultant compressed mixture is then ignited by a spark from a **spark plug**, creating an explosion—the combustion—that forces the piston back down. At this point, the **exhaust valve** opens, allowing the now contaminated air to escape.

That's basically it—though a lot of other parts are required to make this up-and-down motion run smoothly. **Piston rings** provide a seal between piston and cylinder so that the explosion is contained. The **sump** collects the oil that lubricates the engine and the seal. The separate system that opens and closes the intake and exhaust valves is a **camshaft**. The bit that distributes the electric charge between the four separate spark plugs of a four-cylinder engine is the **distributor**. The **carburettor** mixes the fuel with air before it enters the cylinder.

Many modern engines have swanky varieties of these basic parts, but the essential principle of internal combustion remains the same. Your turbocharged motor may have **double overhead cams**, **catalytic converters**, and a **V-8 cylinder system**, but it's still powered by a series of explosions.

GLASSINE is the type of paper that lines your box of chocolates or truffles, and cups single chocolates as well. It is very thin and light; in a special manufacturing process, paper pulp is beaten to break down the fibers and pressed into molds, and then allowed to dry into sheets. Then, in a process called **calendering**, the sheets are pressed many times through hot rollers, thus delivering a paper that is grease-proof, moisture-proof, and even air-proof—ideal for protecting chocolates from that white "bloom" that can sometimes appear.

Glassine paper is used to separate slices of foods in vacuum-sealed packets, which might normally stick together, such as smoked salmon or prosciutto; it is also used to protect book jackets and illustrations in antique books.

The uniquely unlovely sound of the kazoo is formed by a vibrating membrane made of glassine paper.

The **GLUTEAL CREASE** is the place where the lower buttocks meet the upper leg.

If those buttocks are particularly comely, they might be described by the adjective **callipygian**, a word that derives from the Greek for beautiful (*kallos*) and buttocks (*pyge*). The Callipygian Venus is a famous marble statue of a female nude, supposedly discovered in the Domus Aurea—a porticoed villa built in Rome by the Emperor Nero—and now displayed at the Museo Nazionale Archeologico in Naples, Italy.

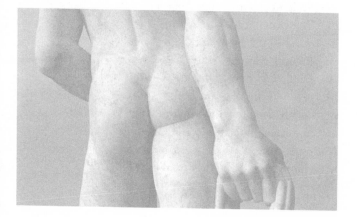

A **GNOMON** (pronounced *Know-mon*) is the triangular-shaped part of a sundial that casts a shadow, the position of which shows the time.

The sundial is the oldest known device for the measurement of time. It is based on the fact that an object's shadow will move from one side of it to the other as the sun moves from east to west during the day. A sundial is believed to have been used in Babylon as early as 2000 BC.

The sun travels fifteen degrees of longitude westward in one hour, equivalent to 950 feet per second.

In the lower forty-eight states of the continental United States, the sun sets first in West Quoddy Head, Maine, and finally turns day into night approximately three hours later at Cape Alava, located in the Olympic National Park in Washington State, a little more than three thousand miles away.

I am a sundial, and I make a botch
Of what is done much better by a watch.

Hilaire Belloc, "On a Sundial," 1938

A **GRAWLIX** is a sequence of typographical symbols used by cartoonists to represent a swear word. *%!@*$! might be an example.

The cartoonist Mort Walker, creator of *Beetle Bailey*, the long-running U.S. cartoon strip, invented a whole vocabulary to describe the devices cartoonists use in dialogue balloons to represent emotions, obscenities, and physical exertions. For example, **agitrons** are wiggly lines indicating that something is shaking. **Briffits** are clouds of dust that hang in the spot where a swiftly departing character or object was previously standing. **Emanata** are straight lines rising from around a character's head, indicating surprise. **Squeans** are asterisks with an empty center, indicating drunkenness or dizziness. **Plewds** are flying sweat droplets that appear around the head of a character who is working hard or stressed, and **waftaroms** are wavy lines rising from something to indicate a strong smell.

In the *Tintin* books, Captain Archibald Haddock's outbursts are always accompanied by grawlix. Some such outbursts are single words—*Artichokes! Hydrocarbon! Cro-Magnon!*—and range from the easily understood to the arcane. The old seadog's longer outbursts are generally alliterative. "Billions of bilious barbecued blue blistering barnacles!" is a particularly choice example. Sometimes they test the general knowledge not just of a child but an adult too. Haddock's favorite oath of "Bashi-bazouk!" refers to the mercenary soldiers employed by the Turkish Ottoman Empire to supplement their fighting forces. "Pestilential pachyderms!," if taken literally, would refer to elephants of a disease-ridden nature, "Pithecanthropuses!" would describe fossil hominids, and "Slubberdegullions!" filthy, slobbering people.

A **HEMIDEMISEMIQUAVER** is a note played for $^1/_{64}$ the duration of a whole note, or **semibreve**.

Half a semibreve is called a **minim**, and half of this, $^1/_4$ of a whole note, is a **crotchet**, while $^1/_8$ of a whole note is a **quaver**.

Notes shorter than the $^1/_{64}$ note are very rarely used in music, although the **semihemidemisemiquaver**—half the length of a hemidemisemiquaver—is occasionally found. Beethoven used these in the first movement of his Piano Sonata Op. 13, the "Pathétique," composed in 1798.

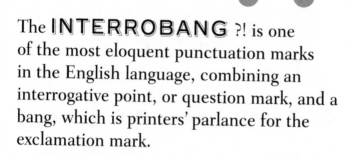

The **INTERROBANG** ?! is one of the most eloquent punctuation marks in the English language, combining an interrogative point, or question mark, and a bang, which is printers' parlance for the exclamation mark.

There are some sentences that require, nay, demand an interrobang:

"She said what?!"

"He ate how many slices of cake?!"

"You're going to have a baby?!"

There have been various attempts to incorporate the two marks into one symbol by graphic designers, but this has never caught on . . .

A **JABOT** is a ruffle or frill, generally of lace, worn at the throat of a woman's shirt or blouse. Jabots were formerly also worn at the neck of a man's shirt, and still are by Scots wearing traditional Highland dress.

In the history of fashion, the somewhat ostentatious jabot has generally made an appearance in eras of luxury and ease. It was a key part of the costume of a gentleman in the late eighteenth century, both on this side of the Channel and at the French court of Louis XVI and Marie Antoinette, where it was worn by both sexes. It made a reappearance in La Belle Epoque, the comfortable, prewar years of Edward VII. In the United States at that time, the fashionable "Gibson girl" would

"Oh, behave!"

sport a jabot above her ample bosom and tight, neat waist. The frills returned again in the 1960s, as a luxe hippy accessory, and again in the 1980s, where power-dressing women softened their look with a bit of lace at the neck.

Of course, in modern times, no one has worn a jabot with quite the panache of a certain Austin Powers . . .

In the world of interior decoration, the word jabot also refers to the parts of a curtain that hang down to either side of the central **swag**.

KANJI are the Japanese pictograms, based on Chinese characters, used in the modern Japanese writing system.

There are other sets of Japanese written symbols, which represent syllables, called **hiragana** and **katakana**. Kanji are generally used for nouns, adjectives, and the stems of verbs; hiragana for the endings of verbs and other grammatical particles; and katakana for non-Japanese words and loan words. When you don't know the kanji, or suspect your reader might not be able to follow a kanji, you may use hiragana instead. The choice of which you use in your writing is dictated by both convention and personal style. The kanji for "I," or "me," for example, is 私. The hiragana for the same thing is わたし. The kanji "I" is generally used in formal writing; the hiragana "I" in informal writing, such as letters or diaries.

When the Japanese language is represented in the Latin alphabet, the script is called **rōmaji**. This is used by Western students starting out in the language and also for inputting to computers. So the Japanese for tea, which is お茶 in kanji, is *ocha* in rōmaji.

Traditionally, Japanese was written in a format called *tategaki*, where the characters are placed in columns going from top to bottom, ordered from right to left. As your eyes reach the bottom of a column, you move to the top of the next one on the left. The spine of the book is on the right, so to Western eyes it reads back-to-front. Modern Japanese also uses the *yokogaki* system, where writing is laid out horizontally and reads from left to right.

After World War II, the Japanese decided to both simplify and restrict their kanji. They ended up with a list of 1,850 approved characters, which has now been expanded to 1,945, considerably fewer than the 3,000 to 4,000 characters needed to get by in Chinese.

It has been said that the Japanese writing system is perhaps best understood as the attempt to use Chinese characters to write down a totally different language. *Kan*, in fact, means Chinese, and *ji* means character.

The **KEEPER** is the loop on a belt, through which the free end of the belt threads after it has gone through the buckle.

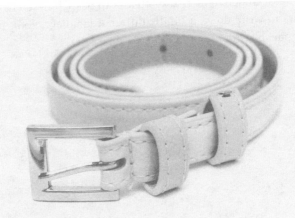

The **KERF** is the groove or notch made by a cutting tool such as a saw.

As the saw cuts the wood, its teeth remove material as sawdust, forming a channel wider than the blade and facilitating the saw's progress through the material being cut.

The size of the saw's teeth determines the smoothness of the cut. The more tooth points per inch of blade, the smoother the cut surface. Most saws used for cutting lumber have five to ten points per inch. For fine work, there are saws with as many as twenty points per inch.

A saw's teeth slant alternately to the left and right. A **crosscut saw** is used to cut across the grain of a board. A **ripsaw** cuts lengthwise with the grain. A **backsaw** will cut both across and with the grain.

The LABRET is the lip piercing your niece just got for her sixteenth birthday.

Or perhaps *you* fancy a horizontal piercing through the bridge of the nose, which is called an **earl**. The helix, which is the name of the outer cartilage ridge of the ear, is a popular location for multiple rings, as is the tragus—the small tab of tissue that projects over the opening of the ear canal.

There's also the **areola nipple ring**, and the **belly button ring**, or **stud**. Some people choose very unusual sites for their piercings, like the uvula at the back of the throat opening, or they might go for a **scrumper**, which is a piercing of the thin webbing between the upper teeth and lip.

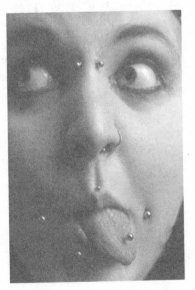

Your choice . . .

None of these piercings is quite so intrusive, nor, one would imagine, so painful, as the **lip plate**, which is a required adornment in certain African tribes. Only the women have this accessory; the bigger the plate, the wealthier the man they can attract.

A **LAVALIERE** (pronounced *Lav-uh-leer*) is the jeweler's term for a pendant on a fine chain that is worn as a necklace.

It is named after the Duchesse de La Vallière, the first of the many mistresses of Louis XIV. She was his "official mistress" between 1661 and 1667 and bore him six children.

In a modern adaptation of this word, a lavaliere microphone is the name for the type of mic that slips onto the shirt or tie of an interview subject. The advantage of such a device is that it filters out some of the ambient noise in the room that a stationary mic would include.

A **LOUVER** (pronounced *Loo-ver*) is the angled slat that is hung or fixed at regular intervals to make up a shutter, blind, or screen.

Designed to admit light and air but exclude rain, louvers are often to be seen on the upper windows of church towers, where collectively they make up the **bell screen**, covering the bells in the **belfry**.

The **LUNULA** is the white half-moon part of the nail plate at the base of the toe- and fingernails. It is a paler color than the rest of the nail, because it isn't so firmly attached to the blood vessels.

This feature tends to be most visible on the thumbs, but not everyone has visible lunulae, so don't panic if you can't see yours right now.

The thick fold of skin that overlaps the lunula, which the manicurist pushes down, is called the **eponychium**, the anatomical name for the **cuticle**; its function is to protect the area between the nail and the skin from exposure to harmful bacteria.

The nails can give warning signs of certain diseases and disorders: for example, brittle nails could indicate iron deficiency, thyroid problems, or impaired kidney function; pitting of the nails is associated with psoriasis.

The MACGUFFIN is the object, event, or character in a film or story that serves to set and keep the plot in motion.

Alfred Hitchcock came up with the name in a 1939 lecture he gave at Columbia University. "In crook stories, it is most always the necklace, and in spy stories it is most always the papers." The "government secrets" in *North by Northwest* (1959) and the "secrets vital to your air defense" in *The 39 Steps* (1935) are both Hitchcockian MacGuffins, and MacGuffins can be detected in other films too: the jewel-encrusted sculpture of a falcon in *The Maltese Falcon* (1941), or the briefcase—the contents of which we never discover, nor need know—in *Pulp Fiction* (1994).

The **MAXILLARY CENTRAL INCISOR** is one of the most prominent teeth in the mouth, which sits with its matching twin bang in the middle of the front upper jaw, or **maxilla**. As with all incisors, its function is to cut your food as you chew it.

Flanking these two on either side are the **maxillary lateral incisors**. Next, from front to back, are the **canines** (used for tearing), the first and second **premolars**, and the first, second, and third **molars**, which are flat teeth used for chewing. The third molar is also commonly called the wisdom tooth, and may remain below the gum or only erupt late in life. The teeth on the lower jaw, or **mandible**, have the same names, but with the modifier **mandibular**.

On a visit to the dentist, you are highly unlikely to hear the full names of these teeth being called out to the nurse as your check proceeds. Instead, your dentist will follow one of three systems of notation. In the Universal system, commonly used in the United States, adult teeth are numbered from 1 to 32. The Palmer system, still generally used in the United Kingdom, divides the teeth into four quadrants—upper right, upper left, lower left, and lower right—with teeth numbered 1 through 8 within each. Your check will start with upper right and end at lower right. The incisors are numbers 1 and 2 in all quadrants. In the FDI World Dental Federation notation (ISO-3950 notation), which is supposed to have superseded these local systems, the first number designates the quadrant and the second the tooth within it. So the upper right incisors are 12 and 11 and the lower right 41 and 42. This system is more likely to be used by the dentist in written communication, when instructing technicians or making referrals to other dentists.

The famous song "All I Want for Christmas Is My Two Front Teeth" was written by the lyricist Don Yetter Gardner in 1944, while he was teaching music at an elementary school in Smithtown, New York. Having asked the children in his second-grade class what they wanted for Christmas, Gardner noticed that many lisped their answers, their deciduous maxillary central incisors not having yet been replaced by their permanent ones. Wisely avoiding the use of the correct terminology, Gardner's song achieved huge popularity, recorded down the years by artists from Nat King Cole to Mariah Carey. The 1984 Spike Jones version reached No. 1 and sold nearly a million and a half copies in seven weeks. Gardner died on September 15, 2004, at the age of ninety-one. He was still receiving royalties from the fun little song he'd penned over half a century earlier.

The **MIRROR BAND** is the ring just inside the main printable area of a compact disc.

It is etched with the name of the manufacturer, as well as a number of barcode identifications. Because the mirror band is not encoded with other data, it has a different reflective quality, appearing both shinier and darker than other parts of the disc. It is not to be confused with the **stacking ring**, on the underside, which is the very thin circle of raised plastic that prevents the surface of the CD being scratched when discs are piled up.

A compact disc is made from polycarbonate plastic; a thin layer of aluminum is applied to one surface to make it reflective, which is then protected by a film of lacquer. Information is stored on the CD as a series of tiny indentations called **pits** and **lands**, which are encoded in a tightly packed **spiral track**. To retrieve the information, a laser beam is focused on the track and the CD player's detector—or **photodiode**—senses the difference between the light reflected from each, before turning this into an electrical signal. CDs hold huge amounts of information; one second of audio requires a million bits of data.

The first commercially released CD was ABBA's *The Visitors*, in August 1982. Ironically, as the CD was being launched,

ABBA were splitting up—this was to be their last album. It's certainly a melancholy listen: both sets of partners were divorcing each other, and the songs have lyrics about failed relationships, aging, and the loss of innocence.

Dire Straits was the first group to sell a million copies in CD format, with their 1985 album *Brothers in Arms*. The rise of the CD tolled the death knell for 8-track tapes and, eventually, for vinyl. Now the future of the CD itself is unclear, as increasing numbers of music-lovers download their choice of artists straight from the Internet.

A **MOONBOW** is the nocturnal equivalent of a rainbow.

Just as there are rainbows during the day, there can be moonbows at night. Both rainbows and moonbows are created by light being scattered inside small water droplets, typically from nearby rainfall—although mist, spray, dew, fog, and ice can also be conduits. Each droplet acts as a miniature prism; many together create the picturesque spectrum of colors that is the rainbow.

Because the moon gives out relatively little light compared to the sun, moonbows aren't as bright as rainbows. The color-receptors in our eyes aren't sufficiently excited to see all the prismatic colors, so generally the moonbow appears to be white.

Your best chance to see a moonbow is to stand with the moon at your back. If there is the right kind of moisture in the air, you will see the ghostly bow ahead of you.

So we'll go no more a-roving
So late into the night,
Though the heart still be as loving,
And the moon still be as bright.

For the sword outwears its sheath,
And the soul outwears the breast,
And the heart must pause to breathe,
And love itself have rest.

Though the night was made for loving,
And the day returns too soon,
Yet we'll go no more a-roving
By the light of the moon.

(George Gordon) Lord Byron, 1817

The **MUSELETS** is the name for the four-legged wire cage that is wound around the neck and over the cork of a champagne bottle.

At the top of the muselets is an embossed tin **capsule**, which some people collect, either as a reminder of the make and vintage of the champagne itself or simply as a memento of a wonderful evening.

To match the bubbles with the celebration, it's always useful to know the different champagne-bottle sizes:

- Piccolo: ¼ bottle
- Demi-boîte: ½ bottle
- Standard: 750 ml (full bottle)
- Magnum: 2 bottles
- Jeroboam: 4 bottles
- Rehoboam: 6 bottles
- Methuselah: 8 bottles
- Salmanazar: 12 bottles
- Balthazar: 16 bottles
- Nebuchadnezzar: 20 bottles
- Melchior: 24 bottles
- Sovereign: 33.33 bottles

If, on the other hand, your tipple is beer, you should perhaps know that a barrel is defined as a container able to hold thirty-one gallons of ale.

A **NIQAAB** (pronounced *nick-cab*) is a head-covering worn by Muslim women, which conceals the face entirely, leaving only a narrow slit for the eyes.

A less comprehensive version, the **half-niqaab**, is tied on at the bridge of the nose and covers the lower face. Another addition is the **betula**, the beaklike covering for the nose, generally made of cloth with a metallic sheen. The **bushiyya**, by contrast, is a veil that has no cut-out slit for the eyes; instead, the fabric is sheer enough to be seen through.

There are other head coverings and veils worn by Muslim women that are less obscuring. The South Asian **dupatta** (also known as the **shayla** or **milfeh**) is worn with the loose **salwar kameez** trouser suit; wrapped around the head, it leaves the face open. The **hijab** has a similar effect but is made up of a square of fabric folded into a triangle, which is secured under the chin. (The word hijab can be used equally to describe the headscarf, the entire dress of the Muslim woman, or a curtain—and, by extension, any separation between men and women.)

Below the neck, the rest of the body is also often covered up by a loose outer garment generally known as a **chador** or **abaya**. In Iran, chadors were traditionally white or light-colored, and black was avoided because of associations with death. Since the Islamic Revolution of Ayatollah Khomeini, however, black is regarded as the proper color for a chador.

Elsewhere in the Middle East, black was the traditional color for the abaya in many Arab countries. In Afghanistan, a heavier version is called the **chadri**— more widely known as the **burqa**; the Taliban, during their period of rule between 1996 and 2001, required women to wear burqas in public. The chadri generally comes in blue, with a cloth grille over the face for the woman to look through.

The veiling of women was widespread in the eastern Mediterranean long before the rise of Islam, a practice adopted by both Jews and Christians. It wasn't until the fifth year of the Hijra (626–7 AD) that Muhammad received a revelation about wrapping up women "so that they be recognized and not molested." After the prophet's death, veiling was adopted by middle- and upper-class Muslim women, and by the Middle Ages, the niqaab was an essential part of the feminine wardrobe.

Whether women should wear the veil, or adopt the unveiled state known as **sufur**, has been an issue in the Muslim world for well over a century. In 1899, the intellectual Qasim Amin published a famous book, *Tahrir al-Mar'a* (*The*

Liberation of the Woman), in which he called for freedom for women. In this, Amin advocated sufur as a necessary step toward social progress for women. He was roundly criticized by other writers, but women were already emancipating themselves, with upper-class Egyptians following the example of Turkish women by wearing transparent veils, and pioneering feminists such as Nabawiyya Musa unveiling completely.

In 1923, something of a turning point was reached when the celebrated Egyptian feminist Huda Sha'rawi threw her veil into the sea after attending a women's conference in Rome. As she arrived by train in Cairo, she repeated the symbolic gesture, drawing back her face veil to the cheers of her supporters. Others followed, and soon the veil had all but disappeared from educated Egyptian society, retained only by women lower down the social scale (though peasant women had never worn it). In other Arab countries, such as Morocco and Saudi Arabia, however, the veil continued to be worn.

But the idea of female modesty in public places wasn't yet outmoded. In the late twentieth century, *al-zayy al-Islami* (Islamic attire) made a dramatic comeback. In part, this was due to the rise of Islamist movements advocating a return to traditional Islamic values. But other influences also played a part. In one recent Egyptian survey, 40 percent of women who wore hijab said that they did so because it was fashionable; and in the United States, they even talk of "hijab chic." Others adopted Islamic dress as a form of rebellion, either against liberal, pro-West parents, or as a form of political protest against secular governments.

"The Prophet himself said that the best veil is the veil behind the eyes. Let her be judged by her character and her mind, not by her clothing."

Sir Shahnawaz Bhutto on appropriate dress
for his daughter Benazir

The **NOCTILUCENT** is a particularly unusual and magnificent kind of cloud. It can be seen only in the evening, high in the upper reaches of the atmosphere.

Whereas normal clouds are found in the **troposphere**, which is the bottom eight miles of the **atmosphere**, noctilucent clouds are located in the **mesosphere**, which extends up to fifty miles from ground level. Being so high, they can still catch the sun's rays some considerable time after the sun has sunk below the horizon, so you can see them glowing a kind of ghostly, blue-white color in the night sky, usually in wavelike, billowy formations.

Traditionally, they are a phenomenon of polar regions,

but they're beginning to appear more frequently in other areas of the world too. You can now see them in Northern Europe, and across many parts of Canada and the more northern states of the continental United States in the months just before and after summer solstice.

The **OCHE** (rhymes with *Rocky*) is the line you must stand behind to throw your arrows in a game of darts.

It's generally located 7.77 feet from the **face** of the dartboard and is also known as the **throw line**. The playable area of the board is called the **island**. Miss it, and you are "off the island."

This is by no means the only slang relating to the game of darts. The **spider** is the metal web that covers the main board, dividing it into sections. The board itself is often known as the **clock**, as in "round the clock." The **cork** is the center of the board; this dates back to the days when the ends of kegs of beer were used for dartboards, so the cork would be found in the middle.

As for the arrows themselves, the **flight** is the correct name for the back end of a dart, which has the function of stabilizing the dart's trajectory as it flies. The flight is attached to the main **barrel** by the slimmer **shaft** and is also known as the **feathers**. There are many varieties of flight, each with a different shape. The most common is the **standard**, but you may also find the **heart**, the **kite**, the **pear**, the **axis**, the **combat**, the **fantail**, and the **V-wing**, among others.

A PEDIDDLE is a car with one of its headlights dark—an increasingly common sight these days, as the high-intensity bulbs used in modern vehicles cause burnout in a shorter time.

A time-honored American family tradition is the game of Pediddle. Imagine a family driving a long distance during summer vacation. Junior is fractious, Sis is bad-humored, Dad is worn out from driving, and let's not talk about Mom's headache . . .

What could be better at this moment than a game of Pediddle? The rules are very simple. All it takes is for the most hawk-eyed family member to spot pediddles, and then he or she has license to hit any or all members of the family, after shouting "Pediddle!" This is guaranteed to remove every last trace of tension from the air, at least for the exultant victor.

The PHILTRUM is the vertical indentation between the upper lip and nose.

The word derives from the Greek *philein*, to kiss or embrace—the ancient Greeks believed that the philtrum was one of the most erogenous spots on the human body.

It's a curious part of the face, because although a very prominent feature, it seems to serve no useful purpose. One charming story derives from a passage in the Talmud, the collection of ancient Jewish writings that makes up the basis of Jewish religious law. God sends to each womb an angel who teaches a baby all the wisdom it will ever need to know. Shortly before the baby is born, the angel returns and puts a celestial finger to the baby's face, just between the nose and the upper lip, after which it forgets everything. The philtrum is the indent left by the angel's finger.

Is it attractive? Is it useful? It's certainly true that some of our most striking celebrities (such as Cary Grant and Jennifer Lopez) have pronounced philtrums; also that both comedians and dictators—step forward Charlie Chaplin, Oliver Hardy, Adolf Hitler, and Robert Mugabe—have chosen to grow their mustaches just to philtrum-width.

PHLOEM BUNDLES

(pronounced *flo-em bundles*) are the squidgy, stringy bits that run between the skin and the edible portion of a banana.

The banana is the fourth most consumed fruit in the world—after grapes, citrus fruits, and apples. Bananas contain three natural sugars—sucrose, fructose, and glucose—giving an instant energy boost.

It may look as if bananas grow on trees, because the central stem is upright and sturdy, but, in fact, this stalk is a **pseudostem** and the "banana tree" is a herbaceous plant.

As well as providing food, the banana plant has long been a source of fiber for textiles. In Japan, the cultivation of banana for clothing dates back at least to the thirteenth century. The outermost, coarsest fibers of the shoots were used to make rough cloth, while the softest inner fibers were kept for the weaving of kimonos.

A **PHOSPHENE** is a sensation of light caused by excitation of the retina rather than by light itself.

Phosphenes are generally caused by touching or rubbing closed eyes. "Seeing stars" is a common way of describing another variety of this phenomenon, which may come after a blow to the head, a vigorous sneeze, or even an episode of low blood pressure. An upcoming migraine headache is guaranteed to produce a fine display of phosphenes.

A PICKGUARD is a protective piece of material under the strings of a guitar, which protects the finish of the guitar's surface from being damaged by the **pick**, or **plectrum**. It can be made of plastic, tortoiseshell, mother-of-pearl, ivory, amber, abalone, or even diamonds. After all, this is rock 'n' roll.

Classical guitars don't generally have a pickguard, as they are finger-picked so not likely to be scratched so much. The Flamenco guitar, however, is often strummed heavily, as well as being tapped with long-nailed fingers, so it has a protective rosette all around the sound-hole, called a **golpeador**.

PIPS are the little dots, or spots—as they're commonly but incorrectly called—on gambling dice.

Dominoes also have pips, and the diamonds, hearts, spades, and clubs on the ace to the ten of each suit in a pack of playing cards are called pips too.

On most dice, the pips consist of small indentations, which can make for a tiny bias, as more of the die is drilled out of the faces with higher numbers. So dice used in casinos have their pips filled with a paint that has the same density as the acetate the dice are made from—to maintain a perfect balance.

Dice have always been tampered with—in the time-dishonored tradition of "loaded dice." There are numerous ingenious methods to ensure they land with a selected side facing upward. If the dice are not transparent, weights can be added to one side, or a drop of mercury put into two linked reservoirs within the die, so it always falls on the same face. Some loaded dice have magnets inserted into them, which are then attracted to a wire hidden in the gaming table.

Modern dice are almost all made of transparent acetate, which makes hiding such dodgy devices within the die much more difficult; and casino dice are each stamped with a serial number to prevent a cheat from substituting a die.

The likelihood of different numbers being obtained by the throw of two dice offers a good introduction to the concept of probability. For the throw of a single die, all outcomes are equally probable. But in the throw of two dice, the total sums are not equally probable. For example, there are six ways to get a seven, but only one way to get two, so the odds of getting a seven are six times those for getting "snake eyes." Throwing a three is twice as likely as throwing a two, because there are two ways to get a three.

POLARIS is the real name for the star we call the North Star.

It is called the North Star, quite understandably, because it appears almost directly above the celestial north pole. For many years now, Polaris has done sterling work for navigators and travelers who wish to find latitude in order to plot their journeys, and has been regarded as a symbol of the reliable in an uncertain world.

Indeed, there is a passage in Shakespeare's *Julius Caesar*, where Caesar, wishing to point out how trustworthy he is, compares himself with this star:

> *I am constant as the Northern star,*
> *of whose true-fix'd and resting quality*
> *There is no fellow in the firmament.*
> *The skies are painted with unnumber'd sparks,*
> *They are all fire, and every one doth shine:*
> *But there's but one in all doth hold his place.*

Unfortunately, while undeniably poetic, the analogy is astronomically incorrect.

Because the Earth has a wobble in its axis of rotation, it points to different stars over time. Polaris is only the current northern pole star. Five thousand years ago, in 3000

BC, Thuban—the third star from the end of the tail in the constellation Draco—was the North Star. Five thousand years from now, Alderamin, the brightest star in the constellation Cepheus, will be the North Star. Seven thousand years after that, it will be Vega, and as it is six times brighter than Polaris, we will greatly enjoy watching the show it puts on in the night sky.

Polaris often appears to those of us in the northern hemisphere as the brightest star in the sky, but that is only because it is in an area where there are few stars that our descendants can see with the naked eye. Sirius is actually the brightest star in the northern firmament—Polaris comes in at number forty-eight.

The **POOF POINT** is the highest point of a pillow or soft cushion when each corner—known as the nib—lies flat on a surface. The poof point is inevitably at its best after it has been shaken, patted, prodded, and generally jzujzed up.

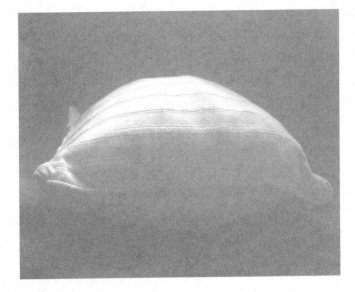

The type of pillow on which you choose to lay your weary head is, of course, a very important decision, and the type of filling is crucial. Cotton? Foam? Feathers? Or how about down, the fine layer of soft fluff under the main feathers? Buckwheat and millet hulls are very popular these days in the United States.

Whichever you choose, it's always worth remembering that ancient and venerable Hindu saying: "The softest pillow is a clean conscience . . ."

A **PURLICUE** is a measure of distance marked by the extension of the forefinger and the thumb.

What could be more convenient than using various parts of your body to measure things? The human foot was the origin of the unit called a "foot," at a time when sophisticated measuring devices did not exist. Lengths became a lot more accurate when standardization of measurements began more than seven centuries ago.

A **hand** was originally based on the breadth of a man's hand, but is now standardized at four inches. It's mainly used to measure the height of horses, taken from the ground to the top of the withers. So a seventeen-hand horse would be sixty-eight inches high. Fractions of the hand are counted in inches, so a horse of seventy inches would be "seventeen-two."

The **REREDOS** (pronounced *reer-doss*) is the screen or decoration behind the altar in a church. It may be painted or carved and sometimes contains statues in niches. Alternatively, it may be a tapestry or a simple drape.

There are other key parts of the sacred building that may leave even churchgoers stumped for words. In a cross-shaped church, the **transept** is the area set at right angles to the main **nave**, which is the central section of the church between the **west door** and the **chancel**, excluding the side aisles; this typically contains the **pews**.

The chancel is the area around the altar, often set up a step from the nave; this may end to the east in a polygonal, semicircular, or vaulted space called the **apse**. In Roman Catholic and Orthodox churches, the chancel may also be called the **sanctuary**; and in some Protestant churches, the **presbytery**. This particularly holy part of the building may also be marked off with a rail or with a **rood-screen** (the word derives from the Anglo-Saxon *rode*, meaning a cross).

Criminals and political offenders in medieval England could claim "the right of sanctuary" by taking refuge in a church, where they would be safe from the law. Sanctuary lasted for a fixed period of forty days, after which the criminal had to accept the charges against him and either face punishment or "abjure the realm" and go into exile. However bad his crime, to lay hands on a criminal who had claimed this divine protection was an act of sacrilege, for which the punishment could be excommunication or a large fine (from a hundred shillings in a cathedral down to ten in a local chapel).

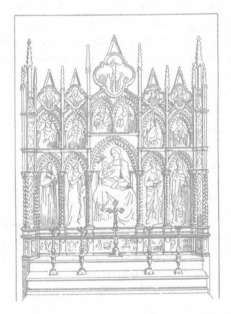

The **ROWEL** (pronounced *row-uhl*) is the spiked revolving wheel at the end of a spur.

Rowels were a distinctive part of daily wear for cowboys in the Wild West of America, both decorative and useful when riding.

Six and a half centuries ago, they were an important part of a medieval knight's gear in battle, but also of the highest symbolic importance; indeed "winning one's spurs" was regarded as acceptance into chivalric circles.

King Edward III (1312–77) was very keen on promoting chivalric behavior. He set up a Round Table at his Windsor court, and had a rowel spur incorporated into his royal seal.

In 1348, Edward founded the Most Noble Order of the Knights of the Garter as "a society, fellowship and college of knights." The order began—supposedly—after an incident at a ball in northern France, when a garter slipped down the leg of the Countess of Salisbury as she was dancing. When the watching courtiers began to laugh at her, the king nobly stepped into the breach. Picking up her fallen garter, he tied it around his own leg, saying: *"Honi soit qui mal y pense"* ("Shame be to the person who thinks evil"). Subsequently, the phrase became the motto of the order.

Today, membership is limited to the Queen, her eldest son, and no more than twenty-four companions. On ceremonial occasions, the garter is worn around the left calf by knights and around the left arm by ladies. On the death of a member, the badge and star and garter must be returned personally to the sovereign by the deceased member's nearest male relative.

The **SAMARA** is the fruit of the ash, elm, sycamore, or maple tree, in which the seed is encased in a double wing of light, papery plant tissue, which allows the wind to carry it some distance from its parent tree, often spiraling prettily as it goes. It's also colloquially known as a key, and some children call it a whirligig.

Maple samara

A **SCARPETTA** is the name for the hunk of bread you use to wipe your plate clean of soup or sauce.

In Italian, the word means little shoe, which is the shape that bread often forms when you use it in this way.

In a survey conducted at the University of Bristol (United Kingdom) in 2001, Dr. Len Fisher set out to see which type of bread was the most efficient in mopping up gravy. He experimented with different types of bread, using a series of slices weighing thirty-three grams, placing each one facedown in the gravy, and recording the weights after two, five, and ten seconds' immersion. The most effective sponge was ciabatta—twice as effective as ordinary presliced white bread. It seems somehow fitting that it's the Italian ciabatta that makes the best scarpetta.

The **SCHWA** (pronounced *shwaar*) is that curious inverted "e" you will have seen written in italics in your dictionary's guide to pronunciation.

It represents an unstressed vowel, such as the second syllable in pencil or the first in about, though such vowels are often found in the middle of a word.

Both the first and last a's of the word America are unstressed and would be marked with a schwa.

The **SPHYGMOMANOMETER** is a reassuringly low-tech gadget with a very big name. It is simply a device for measuring blood pressure in the arteries.

It consists of a hand bulb pump, a unit that displays the blood-pressure reading, and an inflatable cuff that is wrapped around a person's upper arm, level with the heart, one inch above the elbow, over the brachial artery. A stethoscope is also used in conjunction with the sphygmomanometer to hear the blood-pressure sounds, which are called "Korotkoff sounds" (after Dr. Nikolai Korotkoff, a Russian physician who named them at the turn of the last century).

There are two numbers in a blood-pressure reading: **systolic** and **diastolic**. For example, a typical reading might be 120/80. When the doctor puts the cuff around your arm and pumps it up, he is cutting off the blood flow.

As the pressure in the cuff is released, blood starts flowing again, which the doctor can now hear in his stethoscope. The number at which the blood starts flowing, 120, is the measure of the maximum output pressure of the heart (systolic reading). The doctor continues releasing the pressure on the cuff, and listens until there is no sound. That number, 80, the diastolic reading, indicates the number when the heart is relaxed and pressure is lowest.

The **SPLAT** is the flat piece of wood in the center of a chair back.

In the Middle Ages, when chairs first came into household use, such a piece of furniture was considered a very valuable item, and used only for high days and holidays.

At that time, it was reserved for important visitors to the home—the seigneur, say, or the priest; they were offered what was often the only such piece of furniture in the house, and invited to be the "chair man."

The **SPOILER** is the hinged plate on an aircraft's wing, which juts up as the plane touches down on the runway, acting as a brake and bringing it within seconds to a (hopefully) graceful standstill. Fixed spoilers are also found on cars.

Spoilers work because they create an increase in **form drag**—the technical term for the slowing effect caused by an object as it travels through air. In this case, the jutting-up spoilers have made the aircraft's form temporarily bigger,

thus increasing its drag. (Car spoilers, by contrast, have the opposite purpose, to direct air away from the body and reduce drag.)

More important to the slowdown than form drag, however, is that the spoilers create a loss of **lift**, which means that the weight of the aircraft transfers from the wings to the undercarriage, making the brakes on the wheels more effective, and also reducing the chances of a skid.

The third crucial element of the aircraft's rapid stop is **reverse thrust**, when the jet engine directs its thrust toward the front rather than the back of the aircraft.

In flight, spoilers are used to help the aircraft either slow down or descend. Extended upward to block the otherwise smooth flow of air over the surface of the wing, they create a **stall** over the section of the wing behind them, thereby reducing the lift and allowing the aircraft to drop through the air without an increase in airspeed.

Not to be confused with the spoilers, usually just along from them on the **trailing edge** of the aircraft's wing are the **ailerons**, another hinged control surface, the purpose of which is to control the **roll** of the aircraft around its longitudinal axis when turning or banking.

The correct use of spoilers is crucial. The following five aeronautical disasters were all at least in part owing to the misuse of spoilers:

- July 5, 1970. Air Canada Flight 621. The crew were on their final approach into Toronto airport on a clear, sunny day when the first officer mistakenly deployed the spoilers sixty feet above the runway. On the cockpit voice recorder, he can be heard apologizing to the captain, just before the aircraft hit the runway hard, putting out an engine. Unaware of the damage, the crew took off again and reached 3,000 feet before crashing in a field eleven miles from the airport. All 109 on board died.

- December 8, 1972. United Airlines Flight 553. Approaching Chicago's Midway Airport, the pilot was instructed by the control tower to abort the landing and execute a "missed approach" procedure. In the ensuing panic, the crew forgot to deactivate the spoilers. The plane stalled, before crashing into a row of bungalows one and a half miles north of the airport. 45 died, including 2 on the ground.

- December 20, 1995. American Airlines Flight 965. Approaching the Alfonso Bonilla Aragón International Airport in Cali, Colombia, the crew initially programmed the wrong destination into the flight-management computer. Subsequently, their failure to deactivate the spoilers while climbing rapidly to avoid high ground led to the aircraft crashing into the side of a mountain at 8,900 feet. 159 died.

- June 1, 1999. American Airlines Flight 1420. The crew's forgetting to deploy the spoilers contributed to a runway overrun that left 11 dead and 110 injured at Little Rock National Airport, Arkansas. The plane crashed into a lighting pier, broke into three, and caught fire.

- July 17, 2007. Tam Airlines Flight 3054. Owing to a deactivated thrust reverser, the pilots of this Airbus A320-233 were using the plane's spoilers on their own to brake at speed as they came into Congonhas International Airport in São Paulo, Brazil. But the plane overran the runway, passed through a major highway, and crashed into a warehouse, where it caught fire. 199 died, including several on the ground.

The **STIFLE** is the joint in a horse's hind legs that corresponds to the human knee (though it's considerably higher up).

The inside and outside of the stifle have specific ligaments that keep the leg from bending excessively in either direction. These ligaments are called **collaterals** and can be torn or damaged if a horse stumbles or falls.

At the racecourse and elsewhere, jockeys, trainers, and other equestrian professionals sometimes talk of a horse

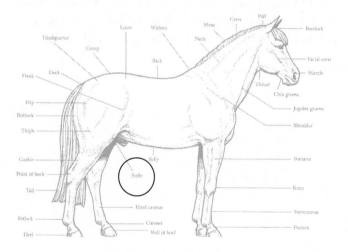

being "stifled." This describes a common problem, whereby the ligaments get "locked" over the bony outcrop known as the **patella** (kneecap in humans). The horse will move differently, and in some cases may buck off its rider in an attempt to clear the problem.

There are numerous other specialized names for a horse's body parts. The average racegoer may know **hoof**, **girth**, and **tail**, and possibly **muzzle**, **withers**, and **fetlock**, but will they know **poll**, **pastern**, and **gaskin**, not to mention **crest**, **croup**, and **dock**?

Horsey people are another group who can baffle you with their complex private language. Taking their animals around the school in **dressage**, they know the difference between a **caracole** (half-turn movement) and a **piaffe** (very slow trot). At the racetrack, they speculate on the fortunes of a **maiden** (horse that's never won a race) or take their chances with a **nap** (most fancied horse). And that's before we've even got to the names of all the tackle they actually put on their animals, from **snaffles** to **breeching tugs** . . .

The **STYPTIC PENCIL** is a short stick (similar to a lipstick) of white anhydrous aluminum sulphate, which, by causing blood vessels to contract, is useful for stanching blood when applied to minor nicks or cuts—traditionally those caused by shaving accidents.

It's a particularly handy item for young men using safety razors for the first time. Indeed, the first-ever daub of styptic pencil—which leaves a stinging imprimatur for several minutes—is a painful rite of many a male adolescence.

The **TANG** is the part of a knife blade that extends into the handle. The highest-quality knives, as used by professional chefs, have the longest tangs, which give the knife ballast and balance.

The tang may be fitted into a slot in the handle, forming a **friction fit**, or held in place by **compression rivets**. When the knife has a **full tang**, running the length of the handle, the two sides, or **scales**, of the handle are riveted to the tang on either side.

The **guard**—or **bolster**—is the barrier between the blade and the handle, which protects the hand, strengthens the knife, and provides a counterbalance to the blade. The **heel** is the base of the knife, generally used for heavy cutting tasks. The **butt**, or **neb**, is the very end point of the handle.

The **TERMINATOR** is the name for the line that divides the dark and the light parts of the moon.

It is clear and sharp, in contrast to the blurry line that divides light and dark on the Earth's surface as seen from space. This is because the Earth has a thirty-mile-high atmosphere, which scatters the light, while the moon has no

air surrounding it. On the moon, day becomes night in a few short minutes.

The moon spins in synchronous rotation to the Earth, meaning that it keeps almost exactly the same face turned to the Earth at all times. So humanity never got to see the **far side** of the moon until 1959, when it was first photographed by the Soviet probe *Luna 3*. The pictures surprised scientists by revealing a much barer surface than on the side of the moon we're used to seeing. The far side is not to be confused with the **dark side** of the moon, which is the hemisphere not illuminated by the sun at any given moment. When we look up at a new moon, we are, in fact, getting a full-on view of the dark side of the moon.

The moon is of a similar age to the Earth, 4.51 billion years old to the Earth's 4.55 billion years. But, unchanged by the development of the atmosphere and of life, its surface retains a record of times when both globes were battered by debris left over from the formation of the planets. Three billion years ago, the earthward face of the moon looked much as it does today.

As the moon **waxes** toward the first quarter, and then, **gibbous**,* toward a full moon, we get a clear view of its topography. The huge dark patches we can see are known as **seas**, or **maria**, so called because astronomers once believed they were filled with water. They are, in fact, giant impact craters, formed when chunks of space matter crashed

---

* When the illuminated part is greater than a semicircle and less than a circle.

into the surface of the moon, carrying with them an energy equivalent to millions of hydrogen bombs. Mare Imbrium (the Sea of Showers), the crater whose main ring is some 707 miles wide, bears witness to a cosmic event that must have rivaled a thousand Armageddons. Later in the moon's life, these craters were filled with molten lava.

The history of the moon—that is, of our human understanding of it—involves many of the greatest names in science. In the sixth century BC, the Pythagoreans taught that the surface of the moon was like a mirror, and the large "spots" in the moon, visible to the naked eye, were reflections of the Earth's surface. The Greek astronomers Hipparchus and Ptolemy, the Arabian Abu 'l Wafa', and the Dane Tycho Brahe all added to a growing body of moon observation over the next millennium or so. Leonardo da Vinci (1452–1519) made notebook sketches of the moon and first observed the variation in the "spots." A century later, the German Johannes Kepler (1571–1630) thought that the dark areas of the moon were land and the white areas water, and that the place might well be populated, by giants who would surely have to match in size these huge valleys, mountains, and seas.

The invention of the telescope in 1608, by the Dutchman Hans Lippershey, changed the picture totally. Though the Englishman Thomas Harriot was the first to turn such an instrument to the night sky (in 1609), he was rapidly overtaken by the go-getting Italian professor of mathematics at Padua University, Galileo Galilei, whose sketches and observations made through a more powerful telescope were rushed out in 1610 in a little book *Sidereus Nuncius* (*The*

Starry Messenger). He described the dark and light areas he saw on the surface of the moon as *maria* (seas) and *terra* (land).

The race was now on to produce a reliable map of the moon, which astronomers believed might solve one of the great scientific problems of that time: the search for an accurate measurement of longitude. In 1645, the Belgian Michael van Langren produced his *Philippian Full Moon*, a map adorned with proper names that he chose to honor the Catholic aristocracy of the time. This was quickly usurped by the efforts of a wealthy Polish brewer, Johannes Hevelius, who in 1647 published at his own expense the *Selenographia*, an altogether more lavish map of the moon. He imagined the moon as a distorted map of the classical world, complete with Mediterranean, Adriatic, Black, and Caspian Seas. Like Kepler before him, he took it for granted that our sister world was inhabited, coining the name Selenites for the people of the moon.

But in this busy era of moon-mapping, Hevelius's version was not to last long. It was replaced in 1651 by a map produced by a pair of Italian Jesuit priests called Francesco Maria Grimaldi and Giovanni Battista Riccioli, who initiated the system of names for lunar landforms that still exists today. Their innovation was to name the features of the moon not after contemporary political figures but after ancient and deceased philosophers, mathematicians, and scientists—altogether less controversial and more enduring. Among these, naturally, were their own names, as well as a few of their Jesuit colleagues. Riccioli is also responsible for the poetic names of the moon's *maria*: the Oceanus Procellarum (the Ocean of Storms) and the Seas of Tranquility, Fecundity, and Serenity. The smaller, dark patches on the moon he described as bays, lakes, and marshes (including the Lake of Death, the Marsh of Sleep, and the Bay of Rainbows). Riccioli's map was followed in 1680 by that of the distinguished French astronomer Jean-Dominique Cassini, but the names he chose remain to this day.

A **TESSERA** is a small, square piece of material—ceramic, earthenware, glass, marble, mirror, stone, or pottery—which, when put together with other similar pieces, creates a mosaic.

In the ancient world, tesserae were used for domestic interior decoration, generally for ornamenting floors and walls.

In Rome, a single tessera (often of wood or bone) would be stamped and used as a theater ticket, or a pass for admission to a gladiatorial contest.

TINES are the individual prongs on a fork.

In the cutlery triumvirate of knife, fork, and spoon, the fork developed last. The knife came first, evolved from implements of sharp-edged flint. By the Iron Age, knives were made of bronze and steel, with handles of wood, shell, and horn. In Saxon England, a knife known as a *scramasax* would accompany its owner everywhere, to be used both for eating and as a defensive weapon. By the Middle Ages, in polite circles, food was eaten with two knives: one holding the food while the other cut.

Forks were known to the Greeks and Romans, but were used mainly for cooking. It wasn't until the seventh century AD that the two-pronged fork made its way into the dining room, and then only in a sprinkling of royal courts in the Middle East. By the twelfth century, the dining fork had reached Italy, and then France. But even at the court of Charles V of France (1364–80), forks were used only for eating food likely to stain fingers. Subsequently, as late as the sixteenth century, they were thought to be an affectation, and people who dropped food while trying to use a fork for eating were ridiculed.

The fork didn't appear in England until the seventeenth century. A foodie's travel book by Thomas Coryate, *Crudities Hastily Gobbled Up in Five Months,* published in 1611, remarks with interest on the odd Italian custom of using a fork to hold meat. The fashion must have caught on, because a few years later Ben Jonson was ridiculing those who used forks in his play *The Devil Is an Ass.*

With the increasing use of forks, two tines gave way to a more useful three. By the early eighteenth century, in Germany, there were four-tined forks, which spread to England and were sometimes called split spoons. By the end of the nineteenth century, these were standard dining utensils. Five- or six-tined forks made a brief appearance but were subsequently rejected.

The fork appeared even later in America, where early colonists of refinement ate with knife and spoon. This led to the interesting difference in the way cutlery is handled in Britain and America.

In both places, the knife is held in the right hand and the fork in the left. But in the United States, a single piece of food is cut with the knife, which is then laid down on the right edge of the plate, while the fork transfers to the right hand, and the food is now speared or scooped with the fork tines-up. The fork is then transferred back to the left hand, the right hand picks up the knife again, and the process repeats (described by etiquette expert Emily Post as zigzagging).

In Europe, by contrast, the knife and fork are held continuously. The fork is generally tines-down throughout.

The **TIP CUP** is the part of an umbrella that sits just on top of the handle to stop water dripping down onto it. When the umbrella is closed, the **runner**, which pushes up the **canopy**, rests snugly against it.

An umbrella is a simple and beautifully designed object. Starting with the hook-shaped bit that we hold in our hands—the **crook handle**—we move vertically up the **tube**, or **shaft**, passing the triangular **bottom spring**, which pushes in and springs back out to hold the runner in place when the umbrella is closed.

Just over halfway up the shaft is a part found only on telescopic umbrellas, the **center ball spring**; this holds the upper part of the shaft in place when the umbrella is extended. Above that, holding up the runner and **stretchers** is the **top spring**, and above that, the **ribs**, which are

top spring

center ball spring

bottom spring

tip cup

connected to the stretchers with a **joiner**, a small, jointed metal hinge. The canopy of the umbrella is sewn in individual **panels** to the ribs—a typical umbrella has eight. Centrally under the top of the cover is the **top notch**; immediately above that is the **open cap**, the **end** of the tube, and finally the **ferrule**.

Among the qualities one might look for in a good umbrella are the comfort of the handle, the ease with which the umbrella is opened and closed, and the closeness with which the canopy segments are connected to the ribs.

The umbrella as we know it today is primarily a device to keep people dry in rain. But its original purpose was to shade someone from the sun (*umbra* is Latin for shade). About two thousand years ago, the sun umbrella, or **parasol** (literally, against the sun) was a common accessory for wealthy Greek and Roman women—men who used it were subjected to ridicule, as it was considered a mark of effeminacy. It wasn't until the first century AD that Roman women took to oiling their paper sunshades, intentionally creating umbrellas for use in the rain.

Around this time, the Chinese also used umbrellas, and indeed the Chinese character for an umbrella

傘

paints a picture of the object very clearly. It remained a device for those of high rank, and in nearby Siam (Thailand), the king allowed only a chosen few of his subjects to use the umbrella.

But in the mid-eighteenth century, in England, the

travel writer and philanthropist Jonas Hanway set out to popularize the umbrella, carrying one with him on his walks around London (it became widely known as a Hanway). The device was a threat to the coach-driving cabbies of the day, who were used to getting good fares on rainy days, so Hanway had to put up with a certain amount of mockery as he proceeded along the streets with his egregious accessory. (Made from cane or whalebone, the eighteenth-century umbrella was not as light as later versions.)

One of the most important innovations to the umbrella came in the early 1850s, when Samuel Fox conceived the idea of using U-shaped steel rods for the ribs and stretchers to make a lighter, stronger frame—the Paragon. In the twentieth century, with cheap nylon replacing expensive silk, the umbrella became widely affordable.

A TITTLE

If you've ever dotted an i, you have tittled, because the little dot above the i—and the j (the very last letter to be included in our twenty-six-letter alphabet)—is called a tittle.

Ever since the alphabet was invented, the dot above the i has been regarded as a measure of something very small. Indeed, in the Bible, Jesus is reported as saying (Matthew 5:18): "For verily, I say unto you, till heaven and earth pass away, one jot or one tittle shall in no wise pass from the law, till all be fulfilled." In the Greek original of this gospel, the word rendered jot is iota, the Greek name for the letter i—from which indeed jot derives.

TMESIS is the separation of parts of a compound word by the intervention of one or more words. Abso-bloody-lutely, for example. Or, un-freaking-believable.

One of the more famous regular users of tmesis is Homer Simpson's good Christian neighbor, Ned Flanders, in *The Simpsons*. His catchy greeting—"Well-diddily-elcome"—is a classic example of tmesis, though whether Ned is aware of this is not clear.

Figures of speech are traditionally divided into two kinds: **schemes** and **tropes**. Schemes (from the Greek *schema*, a form or shape) involve changing the *pattern* of words you would ordinarily expect, as with tmesis.

Tropes, on the other hand, involve changing the *general meaning* of a word or term. The classic example of a trope is the use of **irony**, whereby a word is used to convey the opposite of its usual meaning. "Beautiful day, isn't it?" we say as it pours with rain, but, of course, it's not beautiful at all, we're using the word ironically, to mean something very different. **Litotes** is another form of trope, whereby an idea is conveyed by negating its opposite. "He's not exactly sober," we say—and thereby get across, in an understated way, that he's horribly drunk. Once again, the meaning of the key word, sober, has changed.

SIX OTHER FIGURES OF SPEECH:

Antonomasia—the use of a name or proper noun to convey a general idea about a person. "He's a terrible old Scrooge," we say, referring to the famous old miser in Charles Dickens's *A Christmas Carol*. Or: "You're a right little Einstein, aren't you?" Meaning, you're rather too good at math to be bearable.

Euphemism—use of a mild, vague, or inoffensive expression instead of a harsher or more explicit one. "She passed away," we say. "He popped his clogs." "She's pushing up the daisies." All are ways of reexpressing the rude basics of "She died."

Hyperbole—exaggeration or overstatement in order to emphasize. "I'm so hungry, I could eat a horse," you might say, as you sit down for lunch. The idea that you might eat, even if it were offered, a few slices of horse carpaccio, let alone a whole horse, is ridiculous, but the metaphor works.

Metonymy—substituting the name of an attribute of the thing you're talking about for the thing itself. A good example is saying "the White House," when we mean the president and his advisers in government.

Oxymoron—the linking of incongruous or contradictory terms for effect. "The most intelligent idiot in the company," we might say, of a colleague. And from this simple linkage, all sorts of wonderful extra meaning comes. That everyone in the company is an idiot. That this person in particular stands out. That raw intelligence itself does not necessarily mean that someone is wise, canny, street-smart, or in other ways worth listening to. "A deafening silence" is another oxymoron, as is "accidentally on purpose."

Synecdoche—a form of metonymy: the substitution of the part for the whole. We talk about "new faces" at a meeting, when obviously the faces would never get to the meeting in the first place if they weren't somehow joined to the floor and given life support by all the other parts of the body. "All hands on deck" would be another example of synecdoche.

The **TOAST WELL** is the correct name for the slot in a toaster into which you put the bread.

The mechanism that lifts the toast is, naturally enough, the **bread lifter**, and the bit at the bottom that collects the crumbs is the **crumb tray**. The wires inside that can endure the regular high heat needed to brown the toast are made of an alloy of nickel and chrome called **nichrome**.

In the early days of toasters, the browning of bread in such a machine was controlled by a mechanical clockwork timer; the only problem with this device being that the first piece of toast would be less well done than later ones, as the toaster had yet to warm up. So, the perfect bit of toast might well be followed by the all-too-familiar sight of smoke rising from the machine—and burned toast. Later toasters incorporated a **thermal sensor**, which allowed the first cycle to run slightly longer than later cycles.

Toasters come in all shapes and sizes: the two-slice, the four-slice, right up to the "bachelor-friendly" Sunpentown 3-in-1 Breakfastmaker, which combines a nonstick frying pan, a coffee-maker, and a toaster all in one.

With the latest gadgets, toast can be more than just a taste sensation. The Breakfast-Art Image Toaster pops up bread decorated with a smiley face, a birthday cake, sunshine, or a

steaming coffee cup. But even that can't match the extraordinary CVC toaster, which connects to a computer and allows you to print your own messages and pictures by blowing hot air through a gun onto the surface of your toast.

I never had a piece of toast
Particularly long and wide
But fell upon the sanded floor
And always on the buttered side.

James Payn, 1844

A **TOORIE** is the little bobble that sits on top of the round, brimless Scottish cap known as the **Balmoral**, or the alternative, wedge-shaped **Glengarry**, either of which may be worn as an accessory to Highland dress. You will also find the toorie on the less formal bonnet called the **tam o'shanter**.

Other key parts of formal Highland dress are, of course, the **kilt**, the traditional tartan skirt; the **sporran**, the round pouch that hangs in front of it, used to carry everything from wallet to car keys; the **Sgian Dubh** (pronounced *skeean doo*), the ceremonial dagger; and on the legs the **hose** (stockings), below which are found the tongue-less shoes called **ghillie brogues**, or **ghillies**. Above all this is worn the **kilt jacket**. More elaborate ensembles may feature a **fly plaid**, a strip of pleated cloth thrown over the shoulder and fastened with a **plaid brooch**.

What is worn under the kilt remains a matter of mystery, not to mention amusement (at least to non-kilt-wearers). Not wearing anything is known as going regimental. The origin of the term refers to the fact that Scottish regiments in the British Army are supposed to have worn their kilts in this way. Seasoned wearers advise that if this is your favorite style, you are wise to sew a small flap of a less rough fabric in the groin section of the kilt.

When one kilt-wearing Scotsman encounters another, he is allowed to ask whether his new acquaintance is indeed going regimental by asking the question "Are you a true Scotsman?" Needless to say, a true Scotsman wears nothing under the kilt.

ULLAGE is the space in a wine bottle not occupied by wine.

If the top level of the wine is anywhere in the **neck** of the bottle, that's regarded as a perfect **fill level** for a bottle of any age. Older bottles may have a lower level than this, owing to evaporation over time through the cork; for Bordeaux wines, this is described in terms of the level's position on the **shoulder**, the rounded part at the top of the main bottle. **Top shoulder** is fine for any bottle older than fifteen years; **mid-shoulder** is borderline, and may well indicate a wine that's not drinkable; **low shoulder** is unacceptable, except perhaps in the case of a very rare collector's item.

Burgundy and Pinot Noir are not measured in the same way as Bordeaux, because the wine comes in bottles of a different shape, with a gently sloping upper half. Fill levels in such bottles are measured in centimeters—between cork and wine. Two centimeters or less is a good fill level for any wine; four centimeters is fine for a twenty-year-old bottle; six is too much, and again would only be countenanced if the wine is very rare and old.

Another interesting feature on most bottles of wine, which is guaranteed to stump all but the expert to name, is the **punt**, the hollow at the bottom of the bottle, also known as the **kick-up**, or **dimple**. There is no consensus on either the origin or the function of the punt. It serves perhaps to stop the bottle falling over; it increases the strength of the bottle; it makes the bottle look larger than it is; it's a useful place for the server of the wine to rest their thumb while pouring. These are just some of the explanations for the punt, all of which have some truth in them.

An UMBEL is a large flower head made up of a number of smaller flowers, each with an individual short stalk of roughly similar length that sprouts from a common center. This lovely symmetrical formation is known to botanists as an **inflorescence** and the stalks are correctly called **pedicles**. The elderflower is an obvious example.

A number of vegetables are **umbelliferous**. The umbel seedheads of dill, coriander, and fennel all make their way into the kitchen as useful herbs; carrots, parsnips, and parsley, too, come from the same family.

Another everyday umbellifer is cow parsley, also known as wild chervil, Queen Anne's lace, and keck. *Anthriscus sylvestris*, to give it its proper name, not only produces a large quantity of seed per growing season but also spreads rapidly through the horizontal stems known as **rhizomes**. Some consider it a weed. The state of Vermont has listed cow parsley on its watch list of invasive species, and in Massachusetts and Washington, sale of the plant is banned.

To make elderflower cordial, take 20 elderflower umbels, 1 lemon, 2 teaspoons of citric acid, 3½ pounds of sugar, and 2½ pints of boiling water. Rinse the umbels thoroughly to remove dirt and insects, then put all the dry ingredients into a pan. Pour the boiling water over them and stir until all the sugar is dissolved. Skim off any surface scum, then cover with a lid or cloth. Stir twice a day for five days. Finally, strain all the liquid through muslin and bottle it.

The **UMLAUT** is the name for those two little dots you see floating over the letters of certain words, most of them German. It marks a change in the normal pronunciation of the letter.

In German, ä, ö, and ü (alternatively spelled ae, oe, ue) describe different vowel sounds from a, o, and u, which have no direct equivalent in English.

In English and French, the same mark is used to indicate that two adjacent vowels should be pronounced as distinct sounds, as in Zoë, pronounced Zo-ee, not Zoh, and naïve. The two dots in this case are called a **diaeresis**.

The umlaut is one of a range of **accents** (or **diacritics**) that serve a similar function in a wide variety of languages. In addition to the umlaut, the main accents are:

- Acute—as in émigré, José
- Grave—as in grandpère

- Circumflex—as in forêt
- Cedille—as in soupçon
- Tilde—as in señor
- Macron—as in rōmaji, kahakō
- Háček—as in Háček, Janáček

The generally accepted rule of contemporary English style is that you should use accents on the page only when they make an essential difference to pronunciation, but that if you use one, you should use all. They should be included in French, German, Spanish, and Portuguese words and names, but left off all other foreign names. But if a foreign word is in italics, it should include its proper accents.

Although the English language rarely uses an umlaut, it is occasionally hijacked for marketing purposes. The umlaut in Häagen-Dazs ice cream is a case in point. It is a completely made-up name—the umlaut is punctuational gibberish, but added perhaps to suggest an aura of Olde Worlde European traditions and craftsmanship.

Some heavy metal bands have also favored the addition of the bogus umlaut. Blue Öyster Cult ("Don't Fear the Reaper") use one. And Mötley Crüe have two—but excess in our musical heroes is de rigueur anyway.

VIBRISSAE are the coarse hairs that grow around the mouths of most mammals. In humans they are found just inside the nostrils and serve to keep large particles from entering the nasal passages. In cats they are long and distinctive—and known as whiskers.

Vibrissae are generally thicker than other kinds of hair. They are circular in cross-section, and are the only hairs to taper all the way from the base to the tip. They contain no nerves, but are held at the base by a special follicle that is sealed in a blood capsule known as a **blood sinus**. If a vibrissa is touched, the blood amplifies the movement, and the resulting impulses are transmitted to the animal's brain, where they are a crucial source of information, particularly if other senses are limited by circumstances. Cats, for example, use their vibrissae to navigate and discriminate between surfaces in the dark. The vibrissae of seals are sensitive to vibrations from 50 to 1,000 Hz, and help them to detect prey in dark waters.

Clipping an animal's vibrissae takes away this acute sensory awareness. If you cut off a cat's right whiskers it will have trouble walking straight until they fully grow back. In tests on rats, the removal of vibrissae has been shown to affect not only their equilibrium and locomotion, but also their swimming ability, perception of depth, and ability to discriminate between circumstances. In another study, cats deprived of vision from birth developed supernormal growth of their vibrissae.

Despite this, dogs of many breeds have their vibrissae clipped when on show in the ring; the whiskerless style is supposed to look cleaner.

Not all vibrissae are on the face: a squirrel has vibrissae on its ankles and some bats have vibrissae on the rump. Whales have no body hair remaining from earlier evolutionary stages except vibrissae.

A **WALDO** is a mechanical handlike device for manipulating objects by remote control. It's generally used in environments where it would be hazardous for humans to work.

The waldo is named after the main character in Robert A. Heinlein's novella *Waldo* (1942), which tells the story of Waldo Farthingwaite-Jones, born such a weakling that he couldn't even hold a spoon. Refusing to allow this to hold him back, he developed a powerful mechanical hand, which he could operate remotely. With this and other inventions he became a wealthy man and built himself a home in space.

The history of remote control is surprisingly long. The first patent for such a device was registered in the United States in 1893. Ten years later, the Telekino robot successfully executed commands by using electromagnetic waves; in 1906, its inventor,

Leonardo Torres Quevedo, used it to guide a boat around the port of Bilbao in front of a huge crowd, which included the king of Spain.

The first remote specifically designed to control a television was developed by Zenith Radio Corporation in 1950. It was called the Lazy Bones and was connected to the television by a cumbersome wire, which careless users could sometimes trip over. Five years after that, Zenith developed a wireless remote called the Flashmatic. This worked by shining a beam of light on a photoelectric cell—the only problem with this being that the cell could also be activated by other light sources, so that people found their television changing channels all by itself in bright sunshine, for example.

Six years later, the Zenith Space Command came out. This used ultrasound to change the channel and adjust the volume. When the user pushed a button on the remote control, it struck a series of different bars, making clicking sounds of various frequencies, which were picked up by circuits in the TV. The term "clicker" began with this remote-control device.

When transistors were invented, electronic remotes were made that contained a crystal that was fed by an electric current oscillating at a high frequency. Unfortunately, the ultrasonic signal transmitted was within the frequencies audible to dogs, so pets could hear it and be disoriented by its use—as could some (younger, generally female) humans. Remotes today mostly use an infrared diode to emit a beam of light.

Despite their ubiquity, these useful aids to idleness remain without a more interesting name than remote control device (RCD). "Throw me the clicker, the doofah, the zapper, the whatchamacallit," we say, but to date nobody has come up with a better term for this crucial accessory to contemporary life. May we suggest the Waldo?

WORSTED (pronounced *wur-stid*) is a type of closely woven fabric made from long, combed staple wool. The word can also refer to the yarn itself, which may be used to make twilled fabrics like **whipcord**, **gabardine**, and **serge**.

The name comes from the parish of Worstead in Norfolk, England. After the Norman Conquest of 1066, Flemish weavers began to migrate to England, attracted by the abundant supply of wool from Norfolk sheep (not to mention, perhaps, landscapes as flat as at home). Numbers increased during the reign of Edward III (1312–77),* who was married to a Flemish princess, and encouraged weavers to come

* See **Rowel**, p. 143.

to England and "exercise their mysteries in the kingdom." Weaving continued in the village—and in nearby North Walsham and Aylsham—until 1882, when the last surviving weaver of the area, John Cubitt, died aged ninety-one. Hand-loom weaving had by that time been rendered redundant by the power-driven machines of West Yorkshire.

Worsted yarn woven with silk or cotton thread is known as **bombazine**.

The **YIPS** is half physical ailment, half psychological/ psychosomatic condition: the golfer's equivalent of writer's block, the surgeon's shaky hand, or the construction worker's bad back.

The ball is lying on the green. The golfer takes out his putter and bends over the ball, frequently squinting at the flag and back over to his ball, as he mentally calculates the line.

He's playing a foursome, and the other three keep a tremulous silence as he takes a practice putt, brushing the cut grass with the blade of his putter, before stepping up to the ball.

He stands over the ball—he knows what he has to do—but something, some cursed area in his brain, won't let him putt; it is as if the club weighs a hundred tons, and the distance to the hole, well, he might as well be aiming a snowball at Jupiter. He can't putt today, as he hasn't been able to for nearly a year now; he just can't summon up the physical or mental control to perform the action . . . Tomorrow he may give up the game.

Such is the dreaded disease of golfers—the yips.

The ZARF is the metal holder for a coffee cup (or glass) that has no handle.

The cardboard sheath in which a takeout cup is carried can also be called a zarf, though it's more often known as a clutch. Some people even use the word for the neoprene bottle-holders that are used to keep drinks cool in hot climates (known to Australians as **stubbie coolers**).

The word comes from the Arabic for container or envelope, as the device originated in the Middle East. From the thirteenth century AD, when coffee first became popular in the region,* the

---

* Coffee was first discovered in the ninth century, in the highlands of Ethiopia (still a major producer). From there, it spread up to Egypt and Northern Africa, then into the Middle East and on to Italy, from where it gradually reached the rest of Europe.

drink was served in handleless cups made from glass or porcelain. These were then held in zarf—the plural is the same as the singular—made from copper, brass, silver, and even gold, often heavily ornamented or set with precious stones. Zarf were also made from tortoiseshell, horn, ivory, and wood.

ZILLS are the pairs of tiny finger cymbals that belly dancers attach to the middle fingers and thumbs of each hand, and play in time to their dancing.

They are also known as *sil sil* (Arabic), *salasik* (Farsi), and *sagat* (Egyptian), among other things. They are usually made of brass or alloy and are attached to the fingers with elastic, through one or two holes. Their size determines their pitch or tone, and there are numerous different rhythms for different dances and occasions, from wedding parades to exorcisms.

After many years' use, a belly dancer's zills may suffer from a deterioration in sound. If this happens, there is a simple solution—remove the elastic and *bake* them, at 350°F for fifteen minutes. This, supposedly, will restore the original sound of a pair of zills.

The **ZUCCHETTO** (pronounced *zoo-ket-oh*) is the small skullcap worn by clergy members of the Roman Catholic Church.

The color of the zucchetto (which means small pumpkin in Italian), denotes the wearer's rank. Cardinals traditionally wear red ones, bishops and abbots wear violet, priests black. The pope wears a white zucchetto.

Only bishops and cardinals may wear the cap during services. The cleric will start Mass wearing his cap, but must remove it at the commencement of the Canon—hanging it up on the short, mushroom-shaped stand near the altar, called the **funghellino**. He may put it on again at the end of Mass.

SELECTED SOURCES

Architrave: see *A History of Classical Architecture*, Bruce Allsopp (Pitman: London, 1965); also *The Classical Orders of Architecture*, Robert Chitham (Elsevier/Architectural Press, 2005).

Besom: see *Quidditch Through the Ages*, by Kennilworthy Whisp (J. K. Rowling) (Bloomsbury/Whizz Hard Books: 2001).

Contrail: see *The Cloudspotter's Guide*, Gavin Pretor-Pinney (Sceptre: London, 2006); also *National Geographic News*, June 14, 2006 (nationalgeographic.com/news).

Cumulonimbus: see *The Cloudspotter's Guide*, Gavin Pretor-Pinney (Sceptre: London, 2006).

Gari: see *Sushi, Taste and Technique*, Kimiko Barber and Hiroko Takemura (Dorling Kindersley: London, 2002).

Grawlix: see *The Lexicon of Comicana*, Mort Walker (Museum of Cartoon Art: Port Chester, New York, 1980).

Niqaab: see *Arab Dress: a Short History*, Yedida Kalfon Stillman and Norman A. Stillman (Brill: Boston, 2000). Koran quote: Sura XXXIII: 59.

Tines: see *The Evolution of Useful Things*, Henry Petroski (Alfred A. Knopf: New York, 1993).

Tip cup: see the journal *Notes and Queries*, June 8, 1851.

Tittle: quote: King James Bible, Matthew 5:18.

Umlaut: see *The Economist Style Guide* (Profile Books: London, 2005).

Worsted: see *History of Worstead* (www.worstead.co.uk).

ACKNOWLEDGMENTS

Ian Cairns, Katie Carpenter, Jackie Chorney, Stan Criticos, Josh Dixey, Macy Egerton, Fredrik Elwing, Mike Farr, Glynis Fox, Carlo Giaquinto, Anthony Grayling, Lasse Gunnerud, Peter Hartley, Henry Holt, Rob Jenkins, Simon Jones, Rupert de Klee, Audrey Larman, Aedan MacGreevy, Tina Mackenzie, Keith Makepeace, Paul Manduca, Paige Mickel, Adrian Millsom, Alan Page, Gavin Pretor-Pinney, Peter Schulte, Guy Staight, GT, Norman Taylor, Carolyn Tolles, Galvin Weston, James Wilmot-Smith.

And, of course, Thayer and Jo.

PICTURE CREDITS